W9-AAL-672

THE VINTAGE ERA
of Golf Club
COLLECTIBLES

Identification & Value Guide

Ronald O. John

COLLECTOR BOOKS
A Division of Schroeder Publishing Co., Inc.

Cover design: Beth Summers
Book design: Karen Smith
Photography: Robert Johnson, Harvey Wood

On the front cover:

The cover picture is a reproduction of a Merv Corning watercolor. It was commissioned for the Cadillac Couples Classic 1986 which was a fund raiser to benefit the S.C.G.A. Junior Golf Foundation. Mr. Corning is one of the country's finest artists of the last 60 years. He lives in Solvang, California, and his works are shown at the Youngs Gallery, Los Olivos, California.

Collector Books
P.O. Box 3009
Paducah, Kentucky 42002-3009

www.collectorbooks.com

Copyright © 2002 by Ronald John

All rights reserved. No part of this book may be reproduced, stored in any retrieval system, or transmitted in any form, or by any means including but not limited to electronic, mechanical, photocopying, recording, or otherwise, without the written consent of the author and publisher.

The current values in this book should be used only as a guide. They are not intended to set prices, which can vary from one section of the country to another. Auction prices as well as dealer prices vary and are affected by condition as well as demand. Neither the author nor the publisher assumes any responsibility for any losses that might be incurred as a result of consulting this guide.

Searching for a Publisher?

We are always looking for people knowledgeable within their fields. If you feel that there is a real need for a book on your collectible subject and have a large comprehensive collection, contact Collector Books.

Contents

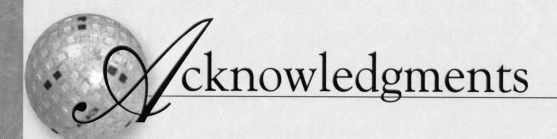

Acknowledgments

The most clarity anyone could ever gain as to the true golfer and what the game means to him is to compose a book as this one which requires the writer to reach out for expertise, consideration, support data, pictures, and sometimes a listener. As one unknown to most in this field, never in my life has a group shown such human warmth, sensitivity, and willingness to share and assist. Some will have forgotten that two-years-ago, five-minute telephone call, and the caller, but each listed below in their own way kept this effort going. Thus let me sincerely thank each of you for the assistance and special moment or moments you gave to me.

Archie Baird, B.J. Blanchard, Kent Bower, Mike Carwile, Merv Corning, Dick Donovan, Jeff Ellis, Dick Estey, Howie Fernald, Mr. Flockhart, Chuck Furjanic, Bobby Farino, Pat Gillis, Gary Hansberger, Jimmy Hill, Bob Kuntz, Bob Lucas, Wensey Marsh, Sid Matthew, Kevin McGrath, Arlie and Barb Morris, Bill Nelson, Ross Praskey, Ernie Schneider, Fred Smith, Bud Thompson, Stan Zandes. Special consideration is given to the Thomas E. Wilson Co., MacGregor Golf, Henry Griffiths Co., Baberton Club, Edinburgh, Scotland, for their permission to use their catalog pictures and descriptions to enhance the pictures in the book or to film their club display as was allowed in Scotland. Special consideration — without the talent and effort of Lisa Stroup this book would not have existed.

Dedication

This book is dedicated to those who have influenced golf as much as any other single group including those who only played the game. These are the very few inventors of golf equipment and the many unheralded innovators who have slowly turned the wheel of product evolution to the equipment we use today. For every "Cash-In" putter or "Lards Whistler" bearing the name of the innovator, hundreds of significant improvements bear the name only of the manufacturer or sometimes a promotional player who had nothing to do with the product's concept of manufacture.

So to Barnhart, Barrett, Booth, Cowdrey, Caldwell, Davies, East, Geer, Hadden, Heeter, Hellor, Jansky, Krauters, Langerblade, Link, Mattern, Prentiss, Reach, Simes, Wettlaufer, and the many I have missed in naming these few: thank you.

One final thought and addition is made to this dedication. This is to the significant contribution by one individual who was such a great player that his influence in the club design phase was overlooked by most. This was Robert Trent Jones Jr. My rating of Jones as the greatest golfer yet to play the game is based partly on his accomplishments in significantly contributing to the technical advancement of golf club design. In this area no one since the great 1800s golfers, such as Park Sr., Park Jr., and Tom Morris Sr. have contributed both extraordinary and sustained craftsmanship in club design with the same level of playing ability as Bobby Jones.

Preface

An integral part of my personal philosophy and an element of my efforts as a psychologist and educator have been the critical and essential need of continuity. Life, and its processes individually or collectively must, to gain its clearest perspective, deepest understanding, and recognize its promise of the future, know first its past and present. Whether of the history of medicine or the history of golf, the instruments or devices used must have their place in explaining the progression and advancement of its craft. As one who has explored the literature and delved in the dusty backrooms and barrels of thrift stores, antique shops, and yard sales, it has over the past seven years become increasingly more apparent that we, for many reasons, appeared to have written well the history of golf during the years of 1919 to 1942. We have emphasized the grandeur and uniqueness of Jones, Hagen, Cotton, Wethered, Hicks, Didrickson, and many others. We have written volumes regarding its architecture, yet almost by subliminal intent we skipped one of the most important developments in the history of golf. This development was the change from hickory to steel shafts, and the clubs which were to follow in the years preceding WWII or 1942. No less than one of the greatest golf writers of all time states:

> When it was first suggested that I should write this book it seems to me that there would be nothing to say since nothing particular had happened. But when under ingeniously persuasive treatment I began to think, it seemed to me that on the contrary almost everything had happened between 1919 to 1939. Let me take the merest preliminary glance at the events of these twenty years. There was nothing perhaps so fraught with fundamental change to the game as the sudden bursting on the world of the Haskell ball, at Hoylake in 1902. But the coming of steel shafts and with it of the numbered and graduated irons was a major event, if not an upheaval in the playing of golf.
>
> Darwin, 1944 *Golf Between Two Wars*, p. 1.

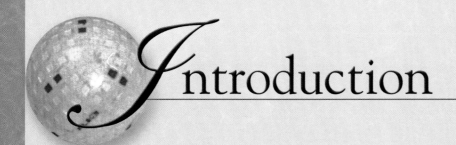

Introduction

The closest written perspective on the area of steel shaft collectibles, that I agree with is by Pete Georgiady, who is a leader in providing written data for collectors to use in the choice of wooden shafted clubs. I believe the escalating high cost of collecting quality wood shaft clubs is forcing out an increasing number of would be collectors, leaving this area more as the province of a few rich individuals. I do, for the most part, agree with his following statement:

> *Many collectors ask why steel shafted clubs from the 1930s have not become popular as collectibles. The answer is they will be in time, but not to the extent that wood shafts are and will continue to be. Early steel shafts will probably be collectible in several areas. Certain autographed models, like the Spalding, Robert T. Jones Jr. clubs, will be favored by collectors as will those from some of the other great golfers of the 1930s and 1940s once their reputations pass from heroic status to legendary proportions. A second group will be patent clubs from the 1930s which were made in steel shaft variety only, never for wood shafts. Today very little is known about these clubs, but as collectors become better educated and as wood shafted clubs become more scarce, collectors will look for other avenues of collecting within golf. The third area which holds some promise for collectors is to study and collect the different types of early steel shafts patented and produced. There is an astounding variety in shapes and patterns which will keep collectors happy for a long time. These clubs will be collectible in the future because they are being discarded at a high rate today and their dwindling numbers will create scarcity by the time collector interest has turn in that direction. Putters, even those with steel shafts will always be collectible. They have been produced in such wide variety that they continually fascinate collectors.*

Collecting Antique Golf Clubs, Pete Georigady, Airlie Hall Press (1995) pp. 145 – 146

Golf's development imitates man, in the beginning, primitive, crude, and barely upright, now contemporary, fluid, and moving in thought and action with force and sweep difficult to contain. Barely able to be disciplined, man has discarded and rendered valueless in months implements that at first seemed the end all. In an examination which dissects the major elements of each new, innovative step, we can identify the common elements it has with all innovation which came before. As I explored and worked toward the design of a new putter, I found that in honesty, I could only improve on old design concepts and innovations, most at least 75 years old.

For my own perspective, I gathered 40 putters, all 50 or more years old, that combined the concepts of a high center of gravity and topspin roll — some with rail design, others of negative loft. All these factors formed in my own design and custom fitted putter.

There are discernible eras in golf, from the time of the featherie ball and the long nose club to the rubber wound ball and titanium metal drivers, from a random number of holes played as a round of golf to a set number of 18 holes. From hickory to steel shafts, from wood heads to metal, combination wood and metal, and composite material and plastics, hundreds of innovations or small changes are involved in each era.

Part of the reason for this book is to help fill a large gap in understanding a great era of golf. From 1919 to 1942 was the period of change from the hickory or wooden shaft to steel and innovations in production and design by great designers — many of who not only designed clubs, but are among the greatest golfers ever. The book will not cover the matches and interactions of the great players such as Jones, Nelson, Sarazen, Snead, Wood, Smith, Demaret, Armour, Cotton, Picard, Penna, Hagen, Gudahl, Little, Wethered, Didricksen, and so many others, but mainly introduce what has been ignored — the metal and pyratone covered metal shafted clubs of 1919 – 1942 and the slow retreat until 1932 when very few clubs were made with hickory shaft.

Although the book is mainly limited to clubs of this era, some editorial license will be used for continuity both by reaching back and forward beyond these years. In general, the reader will find an array of exciting clubs of the 1919 – 1942 era as esthetically beautifully different, or innovative as any other collecting era.

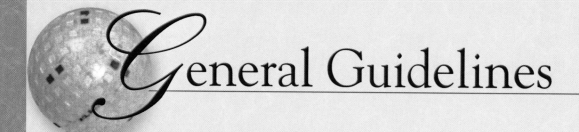

General Guidelines

Golf Club Name or Number

Driver	1 Wood
Brassie	2 Wood
Spoon	3 Wood
Driving Cleek	1 Iron
Driving Iron	1 Iron
Mid Iron	2 Iron
Mid Mashie	3 Iron
Mashie Iron	4 Iron
Mashie	5 Iron
Spade Mashie	7 Iron
Mashie Niblick	7 Iron
Niblick	8 – 9 Iron

Grade Scale

G-10 Showing no signs of wear, circulation, play, or any deviation from "as made."

G-9 Exhibits "as made" originality with virtually no imperfections.

G-8 Minor imperfections and minimal wear.

G-7 A nice example exhibiting all the characteristics of originality, but with evident imperfections and visible wear.

G-6 Should look original with evident imperfections and wear. Still very desirable to the collector who cannot locate a better example because of rarity or financial reasons.

G-5 An "average" example showing moderate to heavy wear.

G-4 A below average collectible, with moderate to major problems.

G-3 Collectibles with obvious major problems such as broken parts and/or replacement parts that are not matching.

G-2 Only the scarce or rare items will have any collectible interest.

G-1 A non-collectible item.

"Approximate value" used in the book is based on a G-8 rating which represents a club in above average condition. Many of the clubs are in original "mint" condition or have been meticulously restored. These clubs would have a significantly higher value.

American Patent Numbers

Patent dates and corresponding numbers for the first patent in January of that year.

1850	6,981	1885	310,163	1920	1,326,899	1955	2,698,434
1855	14,601	1890	418,565	1925	1,521,590	1960	2,919,443
1860	25,279	1895	531,619	1930	1,742,181	1965	3,163,865
1865	48,969	1900	640,167	1935	1,985,878	1970	3,487,470
1870	98,471	1905	778,834	1940	2,185,170	1975	3,858,241
1875	158,350	1910	945,010	1945	2,366,154		
1880	232,978	1915	1,128,212	1950	2,492,944		

British Patent Numbers

1916	GB100,001	1928	GB282,701	1937	GB458,491	1941	GB530,617
1920	GB136,852	1932	GB363,615	1938	GB477,016	1942	GB542,024
1922	GB173,241	1935	GB421,246	1939	GB497,409		
1924	GB208,751	1936	GB439,856	1940	GB512,178		

First Patent Steel Shafts

Mr. T.A. Horsburgh of the Baberton Club near Edinburgh in 1894 patented and produced clubs with solid steel rod shafts which were successfully used. They failed to replace hickory-shafted clubs because at that time the professional regarded them as a threat to their livelihood.

Henderson & Stirk, 1985, *The Heritage of Gold*, p. 91.

It was a thrill to me that through the warm and gracious courtesy of the Baberton Golf Club I was allowed to film for this book the first ever patented steel shaft golf clubs. They consist of seven clubs; four woods and three irons; a driver, baffie, brassie, spoon, putter, mid iron, and cleek.

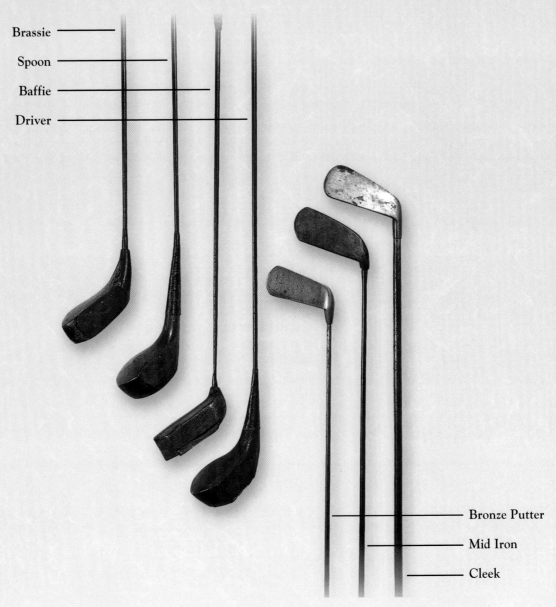

Brassie

Spoon

Baffie

Driver

Bronze Putter

Mid Iron

Cleek

Early Steel Shafts

The change from wood shafts to steel has been documented by many authors. The most common reason given for the change was difficulty in acquiring good hickory shafts and the continuous improvement in metallurgy especially in small metal shaft design. I lean in the direction of Stirk & Henderson who in describing the first patented metal shafted clubs by Horsburgh indicated, "They failed to replace hickory shafted clubs because at that time the professionals regarded them as a threat to their livelihood" (*The Heritage of Golf*, 1985, p. 91). The history of golf has been full of examples of "maintaining the status quo." Overall the grandeur of the game benefits by this steady and slower pace, preserving and lending time to sort and verify clearly great historical moments, appropriate equipment, design, rule changes, and even standards of personal decorum which has as a result dignified golf above all other sports. Regardless the reason or hesitancy for change to metal shafts, be it depletion of hickory, loss of jobs, fear that the courses would need to be changed as the steel shafted clubs would drive the ball farther, it was to happen. A.F. Knight patented in 1910 steel shafts of tubular construction both stepped or cylindrical. This patent, 976,267, included the construction of a torsionless and tapered shaft of steel tubing.

"Up until 1910, efforts to develop and pioneer a steel golf shaft had been thwarted by a lack of tehcnology in the area of steel tube forming." Knight whose original tube forming process involved a copper brazing process to seal or "seam" assigned the 1910 patent to Horton Manufacturing Company for the purpose of developing and manufacturing the shaft. "Horton was able to implement the best part of Knight's process with other patented developments for making the seam to lock the tube. This first shaft was a seamed, black steel shaft which went through many refinements before the company was able to use it in a golf club." "Acceptance of the shaft for use in play was slow in coming since the shaft was declared illegal by both the United States Golf Association and the R & A of St. Andrews." It was their feeling that legalization of the shaft would make existing golf course yardages obsolete and result in thousands of dollars of redesigning changes for golf courses. Also, there was a very strong traditional following for the hickory shaft on behalf of people who resisted the change to the steel shaft for sentimental reasons. Other related and important changes were necessary to accommodate and optimize the use of the steel shaft. The golf ball had to be more uniform in shape and accurate in stated compression, grip sizes and shape were redesigned. Club heads were also reshaped. Special alloy steels were developed which reduced shaft weight while adding strength. "Flex point" or "bend point" matched headweight and shaft flex became an industry focus with Spalding, as an example, stamping their club heads with the following identifying symbols.

○ **Ladies weight and shaft.**
⊙ **Ladies weight, 1/2" longer shaft.**
◇ **Light weight, A or T shaft.**
△ **Medium Weight, T or S shaft.**
S **Heavy weight. T or S shaft.**
⊗ **Canadian or English model.**

Bobby Jones Clubs, Mathew, p. 45.

In the late 1910s and early 1920s many companies utilized the Bristol shafts but the overall acceptance of steel shafts was not assured until 1924 when the USGA ruled the shafts as legal for tournament competition with the R & A finally agreeing in 1929. The competition of Horton, Bristol Co., J Heddon Co., and True Temper had gradually improved the overall quality of the shaft. Seamless shafts had been developed but the perfection of this process as a means of mass manufacturing golf shafts was still impossible due to the cost and lack of consistency of the tapered drawing process. In 1927 True Temper was awarded a patent of their development of a method of tube reduction through a series of "step downs." At this point True Temper began to take over the majority of the shaft manufacturing process.

Quotes not otherwise assigned are from *The Golf Club Identification and Price Guide III*, edited by Mark Wilson, 1993, Ralph Maltby Enterprises, Inc. Sec 8, pp 1.

T.A. Horsburgh Driver
first solid steel shaft
patented 1894

"Speaking in 1952, a senior member of the Club, Mr. James Graham, said that he frequently played with Mr. Horsburgh and borrowed his steel shafted clubs which he found to be powerful and superior in every way to his own hickory set."
Golf in the Making, 2nd Edition,
Stirk and Henderson 2nd Ed, p. 246.

Crest
Baberton Golf Club
Edinburgh, Scotland

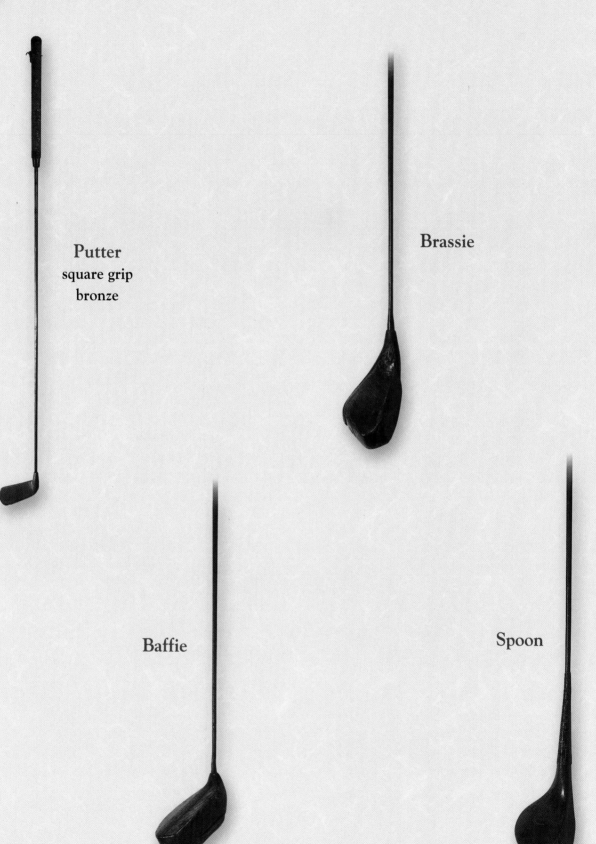

Putter
**square grip
bronze**

Brassie

Baffie

Spoon

Horton & Co.
first American-made
steel shafts
c. 1910s

976267   **11/22/1910**

976,267. GOLF-CLUB. ARTHUR F. KNIGHT, Schenectady, N. Y. Filed Mar. 27, 1909. Serial No. 486,083.

1. A golf club provided with a tubular elastic non-fibrous shaft.

2. A golf club provided with a shaft of steel tubing.

3. A golf club provided with a tubular metallic shaft in which volume of metal decreases toward the head.

4. A golf club provided with a shaft of tapered and tempered steel tubing.

Golf Patent Scrapbook assembled by Robert Smith.

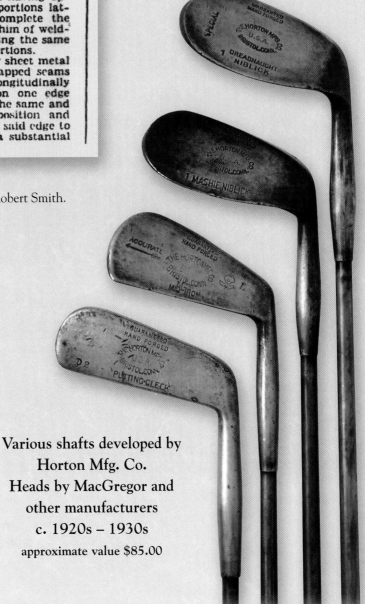

2074986　　　　　　　　**03/23/1937**

2,074,986
METHOD OF MAKING WELDED SHEET
METAL GOLF SHAFTS AND WELDING
SHIM THEREFOR
Herbert C. Lagerblade, Bristol, Conn., assignor to
The Horton Manufacturing Company, a cor-
poration of Connecticut
Application October 8, 1932, Serial No. 636,850
20 Claims.　(Cl. 29—156)

1. The steps of making tubular articles which
consist in, partially forming a blank having op-
posed edge portions, pressing said portions lat-
erally in opposite directions to complete the
forming operation while gripping a shim of welding material therebetween, and welding the same
while said shim is gripped by said portions.

19. A welding drawing-in shim for sheet metal
golf shafts or the like having overlapped seams
comprising a shim of copper having longitudinally
extending means formed thereof on one edge
thereof for reinforcing the body of the same and
positioning the same in welding position and
spaced from the body of the shim at said edge to
provide a configuration permitting a substantial

Golf Patent Scrapbook assembled by Robert Smith.

**Various shafts developed by
Horton Mfg. Co.
Heads by MacGregor and
other manufacturers
c. 1920s – 1930s**
approximate value $85.00

E.H. Winkworth
Hollow, square metal shaft putter
c. 1912
approximate value $700.00

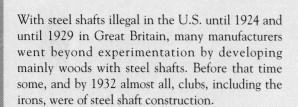

With steel shafts illegal in the U.S. until 1924 and until 1929 in Great Britain, many manufacturers went beyond experimentation by developing mainly woods with steel shafts. Before that time some, and by 1932 almost all, clubs, including the irons, were of steel shaft construction.

Spalding
"O"/Olympic model putter
solid square steel shaft
c. 1916
approximate value $800.00

E.H. Winkworth
second metal shaft to be patented in Britain after the Horsburgh clubs of 1894
approximate value $700.00

THE SPALDING
STEEL SHAFTED GOLF CLUB
(Pat. Jan. 12, 1915, March 6, 1917, Feb. 19, 1918)

GOLF CLUBS

One of Our Important 1918 Contributions
to the Game of Golf

The Spalding Steel Shafted Golf Club is the club of the future. It solves the problem of a successful substitute for the fast disappearing, fine second growth hickory which can no longer be had in sufficient quantities to meet the demands for perfect wood shafts.

The steel shaft will never wear out. Its torsion is just right. Its flexibility, weight and balance give to the golfer the best that is in the wood, with the added advantages of steel.

Actual Diameter of the Steel Shaft

$5.50

Has Met Every Test

It has come through every test of factory and field — many of our leading golfers already have given their unqualified endorsement of its prime qualities for distance and accuracy. Golf players, generally, men and women, will endorse the verdict of experts, once they become familiar with this wonderful new club.

We make now only mashies and mid-irons with steel shafts.

Wooden heads will eventually follow. Timely announcement will be made.

ALL PRICES SUBJECT TO CHANGE WITHOUT NOTICE. ALL ORDERS WILL BE ACCEPTED ONLY SUBJECT TO OUR ABILITY TO SUPPLY THE GOODS. PRICES SHOWN ARE THOSE IN EFFECT ON DATE NOTED BELOW.
PAGE 13—JUNE 5, 1919

Spalding Catalog, 1918.

Spalding
Lard's "Whistler"
two-piece perforated hexagonal
metal shaft with nearly 1,000 holes bored into it
c. 1916

approximate value $3,000.00

Metal Woods

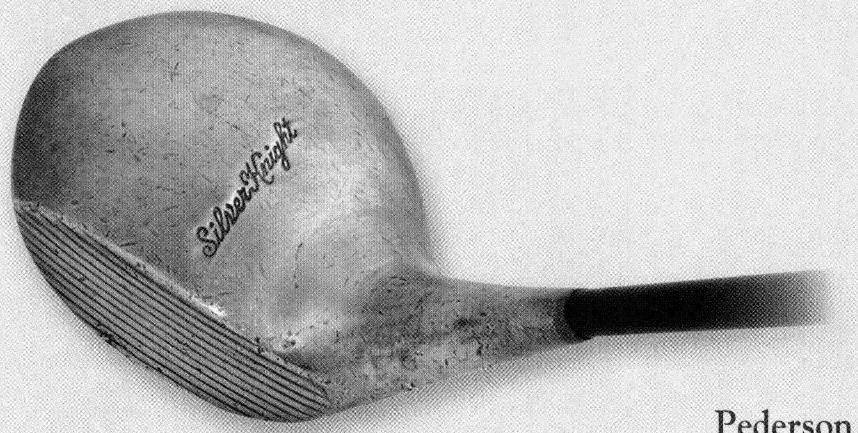

Johnny Farrell used a club like this metal wood while winning the 1928 US Open in a playoff with Bobby Jones.

Pederson
Early metal woods
c. 1927 – 1937
approximate value $90.00

Pederson
Johnny Farrell
metal shafts
c. 1935
approximate value
$450.00 full set

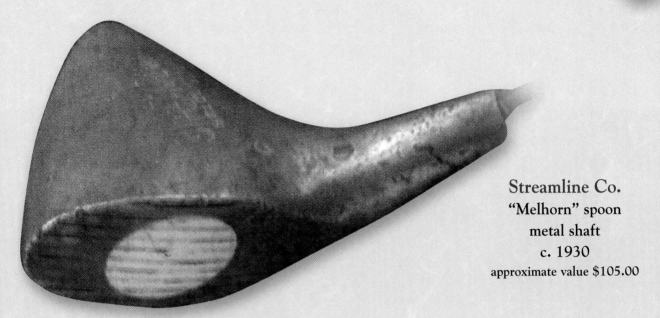

Streamline Co.
"Melhorn" spoon
metal shaft
c. 1930
approximate value $105.00

Streamline Co.
"Streamline"
metal shaft
c. 1930
approximate value $65.00 each

Reynolds
Toney Penna type
aluminum head 1-2-3 metal woods
weight port in the bottom
c. 1940s
approximate value $110.00 each
matched set of 3, approximate value $390.00

Aero-Power
1 iron
"Non Shanking"
"Professional" as markings
c. 1930
approximate value $250.00

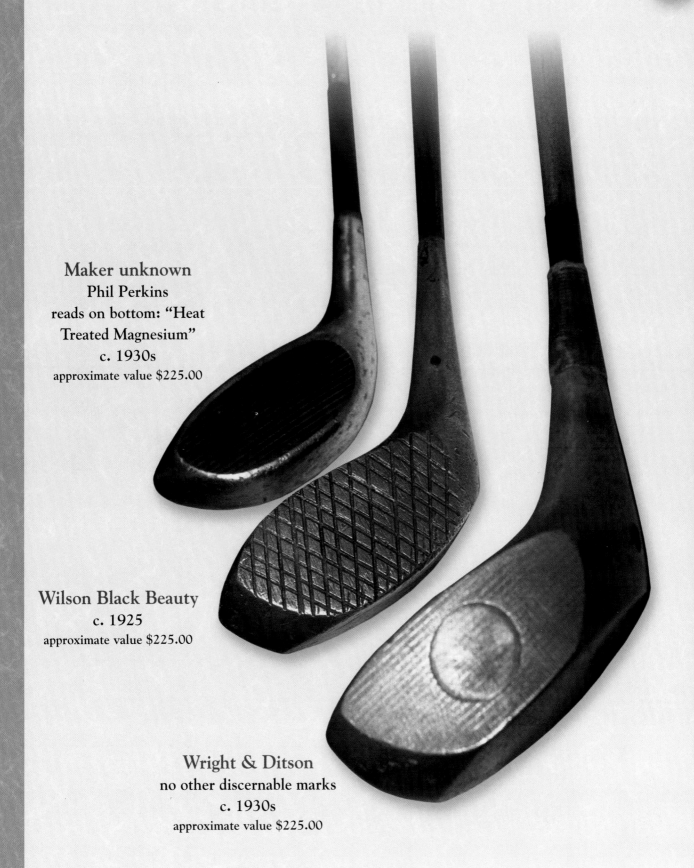

Maker unknown
Phil Perkins
reads on bottom: "Heat
Treated Magnesium"
c. 1930s
approximate value $225.00

Wilson Black Beauty
c. 1925
approximate value $225.00

Wright & Ditson
no other discernable marks
c. 1930s
approximate value $225.00

U.D.S.
Union Drawn Steel
metal wood
metal shaft
hardwood inserts with balancing
weights behind the inserts
c. 1924
approximate value $295.00

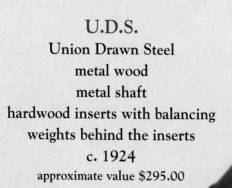

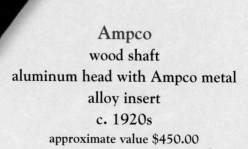

Ampco
wood shaft
aluminum head with Ampco metal
alloy insert
c. 1920s
approximate value $450.00

Aero Driver
steel shaft
steel surrounding a wood block head
c. 1930s
approximate value $650.00

Stan Thompson
"hand" tailored
c. 1942
approximate value $55.00

Custom Handcrafted Clubs
Few artisans of the handcrafted style so prevalent in the wooden shaft era continued in the era of mass production. Three of the best that did were Stan Thompson, Kenneth Smith, and Ralph "Tug" Tyler.

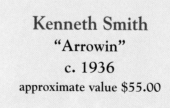

Kenneth Smith
"Arrowin"
c. 1936
approximate value $55.00

R. "Tug" Tyler
Ram's horn insert
steel shaft driver
1938
approximate value $110.00

R. "Tug" Tyler
rear impact driver
wooden shaft
c. 1924
approximate value $225.00

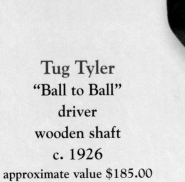

Tug Tyler
"Ball to Ball"
driver
wooden shaft
c. 1926
approximate value $185.00

Watson Shaft
Adapter
c. 1929

Lagerblade
steel shaft adapter
tapered on both ends
in the same fashion as the wood
and plastic ones he developed
was used c. 1925

Lagerblade
or Flint
wood shaft adapter
1923 and 1925

SPECIAL
HAND FORGED
MADE IN SCOTLAND
T. STEWART
MAKER
ST. ANDREWS
T.S. STAR EG. TRADE MARK

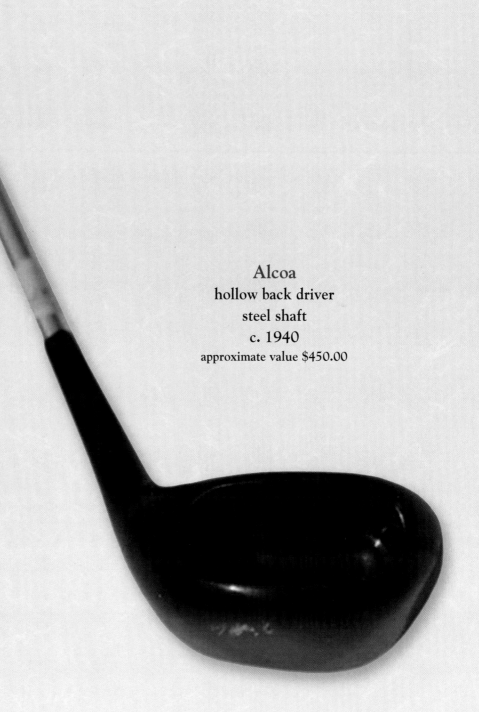

Alcoa
hollow back driver
steel shaft
c. 1940
approximate value $450.00

1600389   09/21/1926

1,600,389. SHAFT FOR GOLF CLUBS AND THE LIKE. Harold G. Barrett, Wilmette, Ill., assignor to Pyratone Products Corporation, Chicago, Ill., a Corporation of Illinois. Filed Mar. 22, 1926. Serial No. 96,368. 4 Claims. (Cl. 273—80.)

1. A flexible golf club shaft embodying a tapered core and a separate tapered tubular protecting and reinforcing casing of non-metallic hard and flexible material of a length coextensive with the length of the entire portion of the core which is disposed between the grip and head of the club, the said casing telescoped over the core and wedged thereupon, the casing and core having contact throughout the entire length of the casing and

being independent of each other, the said core and the interior of the casing increasing in diameter toward the grip end of the club.

1600390   09/21/1926

1,600,390. SHAFT FOR GOLF CLUBS AND THE LIKE. Harold G. Barrett, Wilmette, and Howard C. Bartling, Chicago, Ill., assignors to Barbrite Corporation, Chicago, Ill., a Corporation of Illinois. Filed Feb. 9, 1925. Serial No. 7,817. 10 Claims. (Cl. 273—80.)

1. A flexible golf club shaft embodying a hollow core, and a tubular non-metallic casing or covering sleeved over and shrunk upon said core and extending the entire length of that part of the core which is between the grip and head of the club.

Golf Patent Scrapbook assembled by Robert Smith.

The pyratone sheath clubs, which this book will mainly feature, were a product of Pyratone Products Corporation. The two condensed patent applications shown outline its use. Developed in mostly yellow, black, and brown, pyratone not only protected the shafts from rust but some have advanced the theory that buyer's adaption was made easier because it looked like wood. The green shafted MacGregors seem to dispense that notion. One drawback realized rather quickly was that they were, contrary to advertised, susceptible to chipping and peeling where the hosel met the shaft. Without question they required care after use and in the bag.

It is tempting as a writer to jump into the fray which would occur if one confronted the mindset of those who feel that only if the club has a wood handle it is of value or collector status. One does not always challenge rarity, uniqueness, and craftsmanship as an index of value, but three matched MacGregor Chieftians side by side, all equal other than wood shafts in one set and perfect pyratone sheating on the second set of shafts, does not to me add value differentiation. I have known awe and almost reverence as I've held and examined a Dickson, Cossar, Phillip, Morris, Jackson, Park, and others of unquestioned magnificence in my hand, yet for those clubs caught in the transition of wood to metal such as the Yardsmore putter shown in the book (page 144), the only difference being that the metal shafted one is better constructed, I would stand my ground as to its value equivalency. One would offer a second brief explanation of the sideways look by those who carelessly perpetuate the myth of "there's millions of them still out there." Any theory of disuse, discard, or rapid evolution of an expendable product confronts this concept on its face. Those of us, heavy in the search, would clearly ask the myth maker "where are they out there?" Many I have spoke with who search out and sell golf items cleary testify to the significant decrease in the sheathed or painted shaft clubs of the 1920 – 1942 era. Their increasing costs also bear this out. Leave out these with shattered or badly damaged shafts, those whose grips have been removed to use on wooden shafts, and leaving the one common single pyratone shaft in the barrel, and your search can be fairly empty. Some of these clubs are now approaching the 100 year mark, represent another century, and if carefully selected, give the collector an opportunity to own meaningful symbols of great players, inventors, companies, at as yet sensible prices.

Harry Vardon
Totteridge
London, England
copper coated shaft
c. 1927
approximate value $135.00

D Anderson & Sons
St. Andrews
"Highland"
copper coated shaft
c. 1927
approximate value $135.00

Wilson
Aero-Flo-Turfrider
steel shaft
c. 1939
approximate value $25.00

McGill Mfg. Co.
"The Seventy One" driver
large persimmon head
c. 1937
approximate value $45.00

MacGregor
wood shafted
"BAP"
Bulger Brassie
c. 1921
approximate value $85.00

Bristol Driver
steel shaft
steel sweet spot insert
c. 1930s
approximate value $45.00

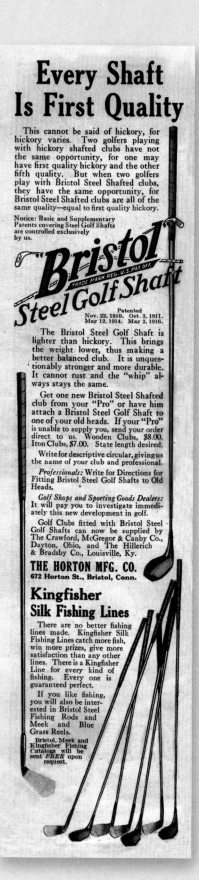

Every Shaft Is First Quality

This cannot be said of hickory, for hickory varies. Two golfers playing with hickory shafted clubs have not the same opportunity, for one may have first quality hickory and the other fifth quality. But when two golfers play with Bristol Steel Shafted clubs, they have the same opportunity, for Bristol Steel Shafted clubs are all of the same quality—equal to first quality hickory.

Notice: Basic and Supplementary Patents covering Steel Golf Shafts are controlled exclusively by us.

Bristol Steel Golf Shaft

Patented
Nov. 22, 1910. Oct. 3, 1911.
May 12, 1914. May 2, 1916.

The Bristol Steel Golf Shaft is lighter than hickory. This brings the weight lower, thus making a better balanced club. It is unquestionably stronger and more durable. It cannot rust and the "whip" always stays the same.

Get one new Bristol Steel Shafted club from your "Pro" or have him attach a Bristol Steel Golf Shaft to one of your old heads. If your "Pro" is unable to supply you, send your order direct to us. Wooden Clubs, $8.00. Iron Clubs, $7.00. State length desired.

Write for descriptive circular, giving us the name of your club and professional.

Professionals: Write for Directions for Fitting Bristol Steel Golf Shafts to Old Heads.

Golf Shops and Sporting Goods Dealers: It will pay you to investigate immediately this new development in golf.

Golf Clubs fitted with Bristol Steel Golf Shafts can now be supplied by The Crawford, McGregor & Canby Co., Dayton, Ohio, and The Hillerich & Bradsby Co., Louisville, Ky.

THE HORTON MFG. CO.
672 Horton St., Bristol, Conn.

Kingfisher Silk Fishing Lines

There are no better fishing lines made. Kingfisher Silk Fishing Lines catch more fish, win more prizes, give more satisfaction than any other lines. There is a Kingfisher Line for every kind of fishing. Every one is guaranteed perfect.

If you like fishing, you will also be interested in Bristol Steel Fishing Rods and Meek and Blue Grass Reels.

Bristol, Meek and Kingfisher Fishing Catalogs will be sent *FREE* upon request.

1922 Bristol ad

1922 MacGregor ad

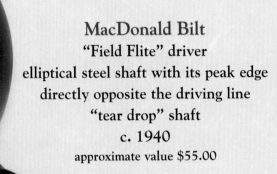

MacDonald Bilt
"Field Flite" driver
elliptical steel shaft with its peak edge
directly opposite the driving line
"tear drop" shaft
c. 1940
approximate value $55.00

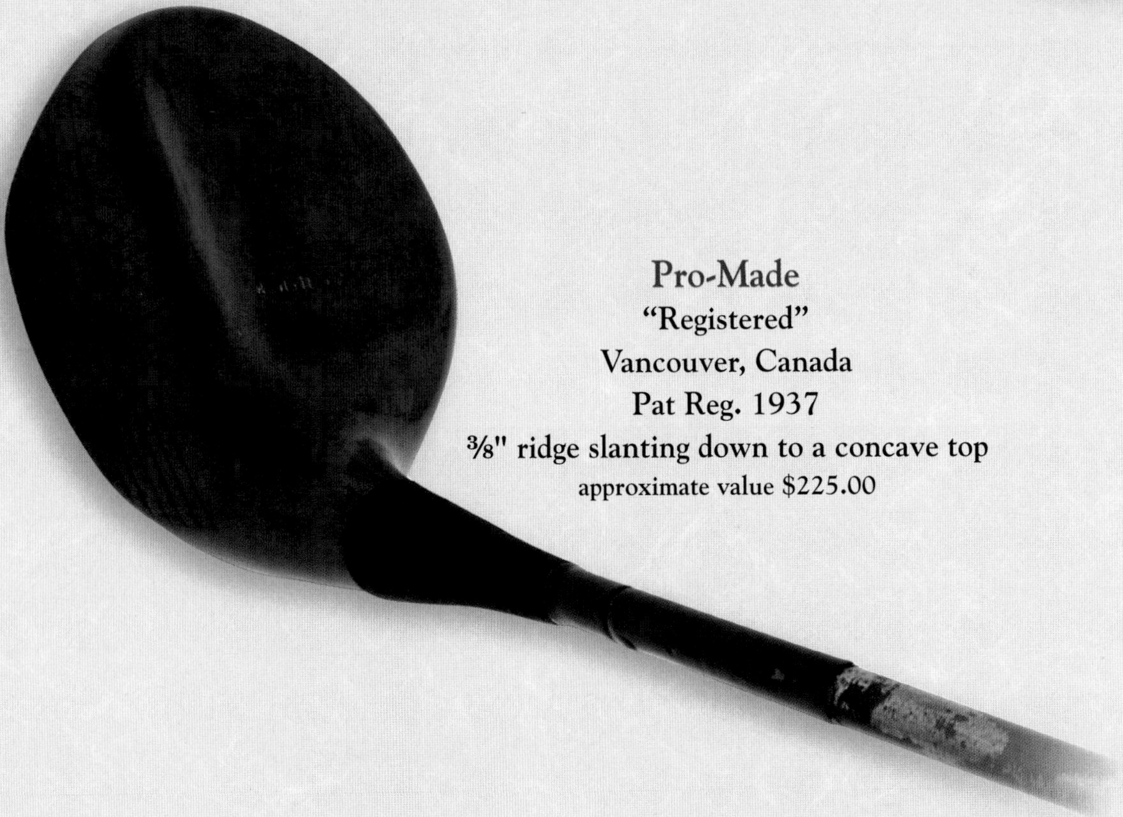

Pro-Made
"Registered"
Vancouver, Canada
Pat Reg. 1937
⅜" ridge slanting down to a concave top
approximate value $225.00

Sid Green
"Peak Hi" driver
wood shaft
c. 1932
approximate value $635.00

Unknown maker
no markings
The wine colored wood is more tapered.
Both show visible evidence of play.
They may be prototypes.
c. 1940s
approximate value $250.00 each

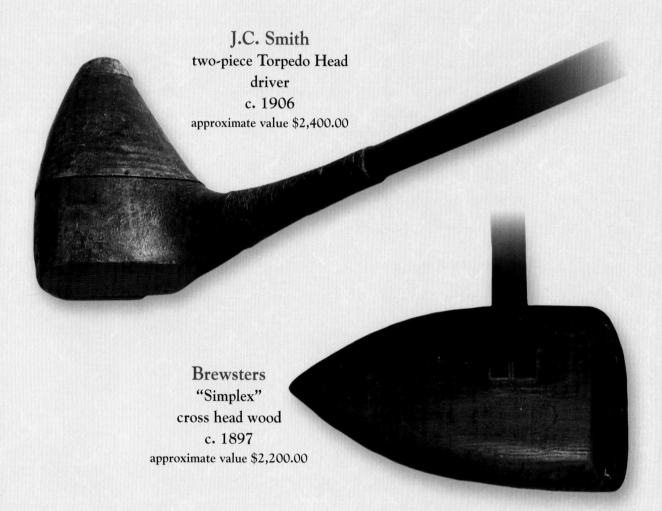

J.C. Smith
two-piece Torpedo Head
driver
c. 1906
approximate value $2,400.00

Brewsters
"Simplex"
cross head wood
c. 1897
approximate value $2,200.00

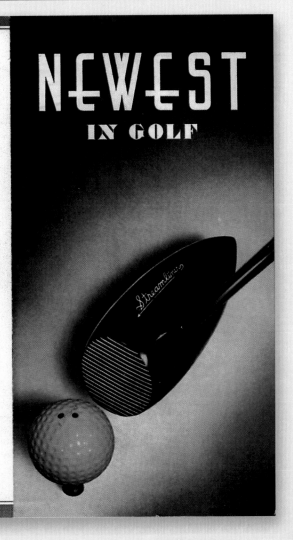

THE NEW *and* THE OLD

THE NEW "Streamliner" woods will drive the golf ball from 15 to 20 yards farther than the OLD traditional woods.

The NEW "Streamliner" golf club has only one-tenth as much air resistance as the OLD style club.

The NEW "Streamliner" design locates the weight of the club head directly behind the impact center, while the weight in the OLD head is unsymmetrical and unbalanced.

The NEW "Streamliner" design is specified by aerodynamic science, while the OLD "jest growed" like "Topsy".

If your hunting is done with a rifle, try the NEW "Streamliner". If you hunt with a "blunder-buss" stick to the OLD.

The NEW "Streamliner" is MADE BY MACGREGOR CRAFTSMEN.

MacGregor made
Crooker patent
"Streamliner"
Illegal yet produced in 1937.
They were an ideal example of
"don't drink when driving," short-
lived as a desirable golf club.
c. 1937
approximate value $225.00

Volkman
"Glider" driver
concave and beveled top
pyratone shaft
c. 1930s
approximate value $125.00

Jack White
"Sit Rite"
concave toe-tapered sole
c. 1920s
approximate value $125.00

Hattstrom
"Can't Miss" on top
Gourley "Golf Masters" on
bottom plate
c. 1940s
approximate value $450.00

Unknown maker
horse hoof driver
c. 1930
approximate value $300.00

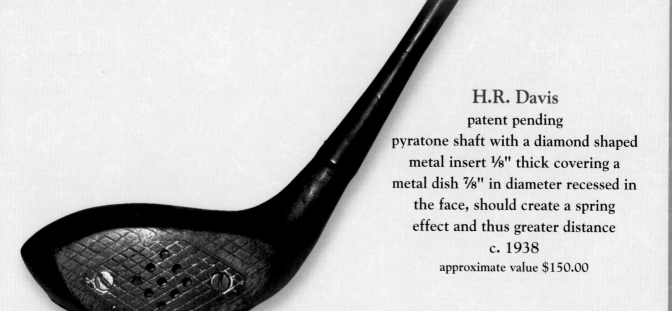

H.R. Davis
patent pending
pyratone shaft with a diamond shaped
metal insert ⅛" thick covering a
metal dish ⅞" in diameter recessed in
the face, should create a spring
effect and thus greater distance
c. 1938
approximate value $150.00

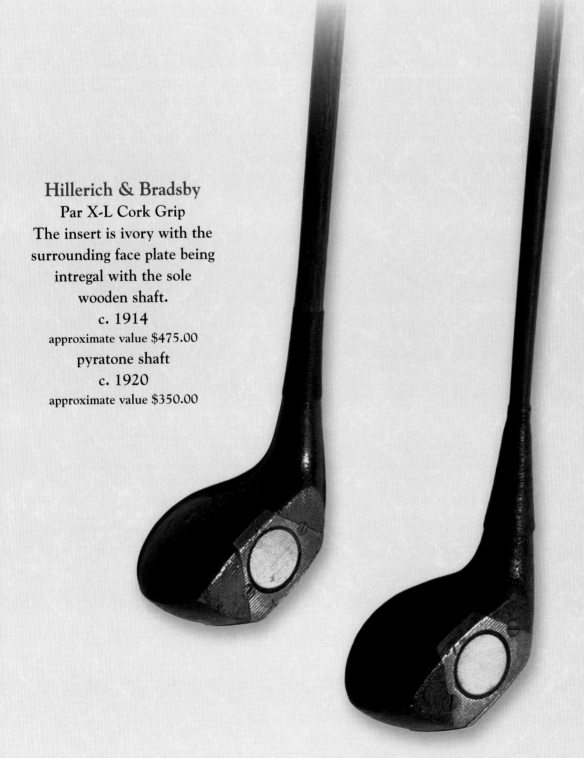

Hillerich & Bradsby
Par X-L Cork Grip
The insert is ivory with the
surrounding face plate being
intregal with the sole
wooden shaft.
c. 1914
approximate value $475.00
pyratone shaft
c. 1920
approximate value $350.00

GREAT DESIGN FEATURES
FOUND IN MACGREGOR CLUBS

When a MacGregor Player-Craftsman dubs a shot, he talks right out loud—just like any other golfer. And when he dubs several in a row, he commences to talk about his clubs—also just like any other golfer!

And that's the way most of the MacGregor patented features originated. To be sure, MacGregor engineers and the experimental laboratory are always available for help, but the Golf Course is where inventions are born.

Upon the MacGregor Course and by the MacGregor Player-Craftsmen, the first steel shafts were tested and developed, as were many other of the most important improvements ever contributed to golf.

The most recent ones, as described in this catalog, were perfected to aid you in playing a more enjoyable game of golf. They are not just so many gadgets devised to make advertising copy, but they have the unqualified approval of the entire MacGregor Clan.

THE VICKERY MASTER SHAFT

True Temper and MacGregor Player-Craftsmen collaborated with Mr. Norman Vickery, Professional at the Pine Valley Club in Massachusetts, in developing this shaft.

MacGregor Craftsmen of the pre-steel-shaft era endeavored to put into each club the shaft of specific stiffness best suited to the shot to be played. They carefully sanded and waggled each club as they made it, so that the flexing area was exactly in the correct position for maximum distance and controllability. This accounted for what was often termed the "sweet feel" of hickory shafts.

The Master Steel Shaft is built upon this same principle. By mathematical calculation, and through playing tests, the proper leverage points are ascertained. A section of slightly smaller diameter, stiffened both above and below by step sections, results in the Controlled Flex Area. This area is graduated in relation to the type of club, being placed high on distance clubs and lower on approaching clubs which must be played firmly.

GRIEVE TURFLO HEAD

As shown in the illustration, the sole of this club barely touches the turf, which allows the club head to come through the shot without deflection.

This extremely narrow drag area is particularly effective on the fairway where difficult lies are frequent. Driver, Brassie, Spoon, or No. 4 may be played with equal facility, the shorter clubs negotiating bad lies and taking the ball out cleanly.

Because of the removal of excess wood at heel and toe, additional lead is applied in the back directly behind the point of impact, giving the head unusual power and distance.

The rocking lie of the head also makes it readily adaptable to the normal stance of most golfers.

Designed and patented by Mr. Fred Grieve, a prominent New York Professional, the Turflo Head was thoroughly tested and improved by MacGregor Player-Craftsmen. It may be said to be the first and only wood not designed by this group to have their entire approval.

THE CONTROL SLEEVE

The function of the MacGregor Control Sleeve is to keep flexibility out of the grip and in the Whip Control Section. This sleeve fits over the steel shaft and stiffens it under the grip, putting the leverage where it belongs.

THE NEUTRALIZER

The MacGregor Neutralizer is a section of tough, springy hickory that fits *inside* the steel shaft where it joins the club head. It gives rigidity and strength at the neck where it is vitally needed. It serves to absorb shock and vibration which otherwise would be carried up the shaft to the hands. Breakage is thereby eliminated as proved by the fact that no club equipped with the Neutralizer has ever broken at the neck.

Page 1, 1936 Golf

Courtesy Crawford, MacGregor, and Canby Company.

MacGregor
beveled sole
c. 1935
approximate value $105.00

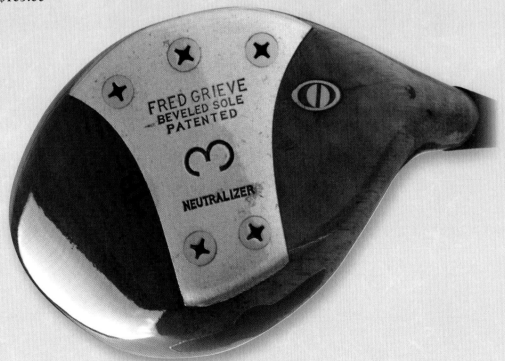

MacGregor
Pace-maker
P-4M
Tur-flo Model head
neutralizer shaft
Mac-oid covered shaft
No lap calf-skin grip
c. 1935
Restored: approximate value $115.00

Wilson
sole-numbered woods
c. 1930s
approximate value $255.00 set

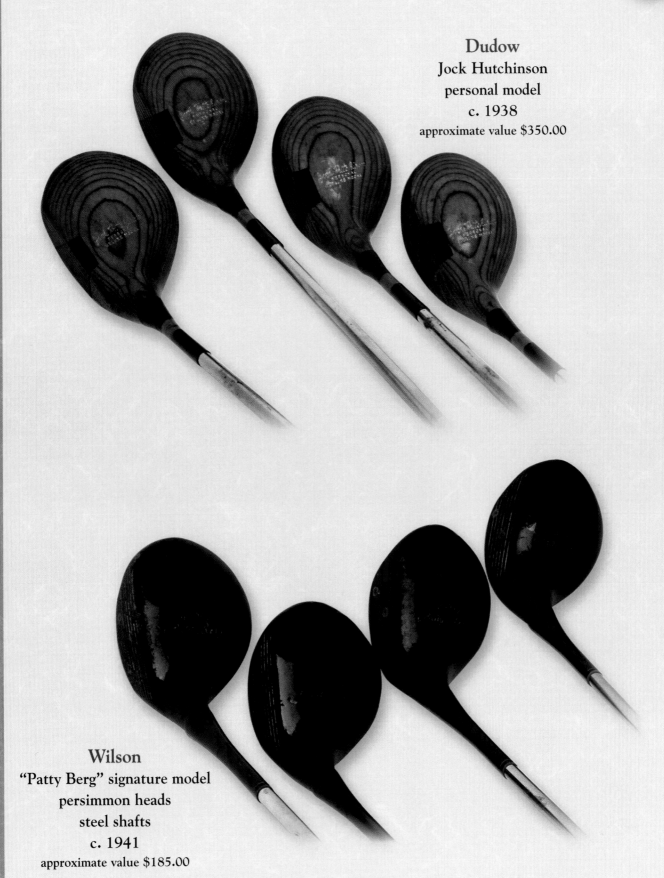

Dudow
Jock Hutchinson
personal model
c. 1938
approximate value $350.00

Wilson
"Patty Berg" signature model
persimmon heads
steel shafts
c. 1941
approximate value $185.00

Wilson
Gene Sarazen 4-star
c. 1930s
approximate value $175.00 set

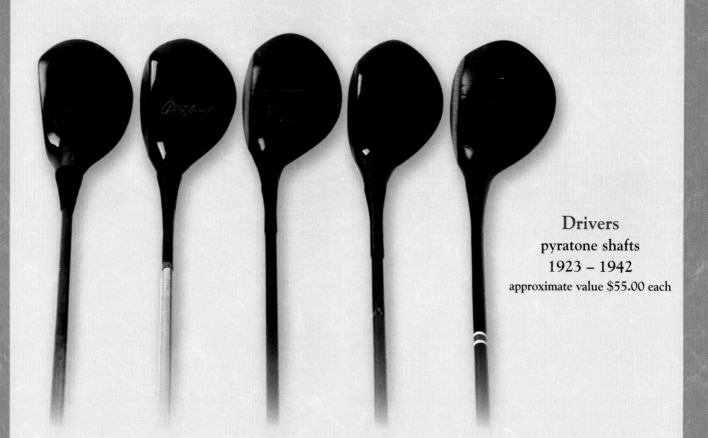

Drivers
pyratone shafts
1923 – 1942
approximate value $55.00 each

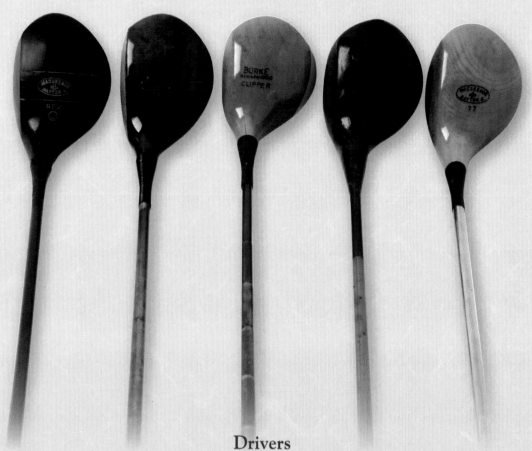

Drivers
pyratone and steel shafted
c. 1923 – 1938
approximate value $55.00 each

Brassies or 2 Woods
pyratone and steel shafts
c. 1923 – 1938
approximate value $55.00 each

Spoons or 3 Woods
pyratone and steel shafted
c. 1929 – 1940
approximate value $55.00 each

Spalding
Fancy Face
5 Woods
c. 1923
approximate value $85.00 each

Wilson "Turf Riders"
concave bottom
c. 1935
approximate value $125.00 set

Made famous when Sarazen used a Turf Rider Spoon to hit his famous double eagle to help win the 1935 Masters.

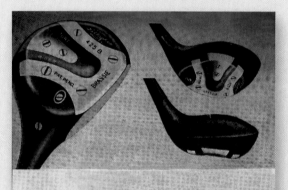

NEW JIM GALLAGHER

The New Jim Gallagher Turf Rider is a real achievement in the development of wood clubs. First, it is a fine model of what experts claim a golf club should be —the balance and power alone make it attractive. In addition to this the sole has been scooped out, creating a concave opening at the back of the club, which gradually diminishes toward the front until with one-quarter of an inch from the face it becomes flush with the balance of the sole.

On either side of this concavity a specially designed sole plate, which does not extend above the general surface of the sole itself, gives the effect of runners.

PAGE 3, 1935 PROFESSIONAL

Courtesy the T.E. Wilson Company.

Tooley & Sons
wooden shaft
c. 1920s
approximate value $350.00

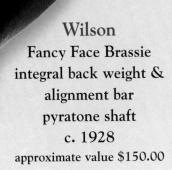

Wilson
Fancy Face Brassie
integral back weight &
alignment bar
pyratone shaft
c. 1928
approximate value $150.00

Wilson
Fancy Face "Crest" driver
integral back weight &
alignment bar
pyratone shaft
c. 1927
approximate value $150.00

Waverly Horton
Wonder Club
c. 1920
approximate value $225.00

Wilson
"Sharpshooter"
pyratone shaft
c. 1920
approximate value $210.00

Unknown maker
metal casing
wood head & face
c. 1930
approximate value $210.00

Niagra
metal wood
hard plastic top
c. 1930s
approximate value $210.00

MacGregor
Parmaker
Ben Hogan
Dick Metz Turflo sole plate
c. 1940
approximate value $80.00

D. Ogilvie
"Pick Up" wood
c. 1920
approximate value $250.00

Cann & Taylor
"Confidus Spoon"
ridge sole
c. 1920s
approximate value $250.00

Jack White
driver
London
pyratone shaft
c. 1928
approximate value $145.00

Wilson
"Fore Master"
diamond wood inset
c. 1939
approximate value $40.00

Walter Hagan
"Crested Head" driver
steel shaft
c. 1930s
approximate value $150.00

*I*rons and Full Sets

Born in 1856, George Loew was a golf professional and famous golf course designer. He patented, in 1896, a set of irons resembling the Farrlie anti-shank design. They measured 3" wide with a breadth of 1⅜", the only difference being in loft. Although years later such club makers as Standard Golf, Nicoll, Spalding, MacGregor, and Wilson have advertised their "new" clubs as the first to develop a "matched set," Lowe's set of irons with the "all hitting face" or "flat irons" would have to be viewed as the forerunner of this concept.

The niblick shown below left is the same width but larger in breadth than the uniform size of 1⅜" the other clubs measured, however "when placed behind the ball the of the top niblicks face like the top of each of the other club faces is only 1⅜" inches above the ground. Because of its considerable loft the niblicks blade need more surface area to reach the same elevation" (*The Clubmakers Art*, 1997: 169).

Peter Georgiady's comments in *View and Reviews* contain the following quote regarding these clubs "George Lowe of St. Annes on Sea has achieved considerable success with his patent irons. They are all one shape and size but corresponding laid back to form mashie irons and cleeks, each club having an all hitting face. Though these clubs have found their way in many a foreign parcel, on shippers instructions probably, the club which appeals to the bulk of golfers is George Lowe's "Niblick." Made on the all hitting principle it is undoubtedly one of the finest niblicks in use. Results have proved to be so (*Golfing*, July 11, 01).

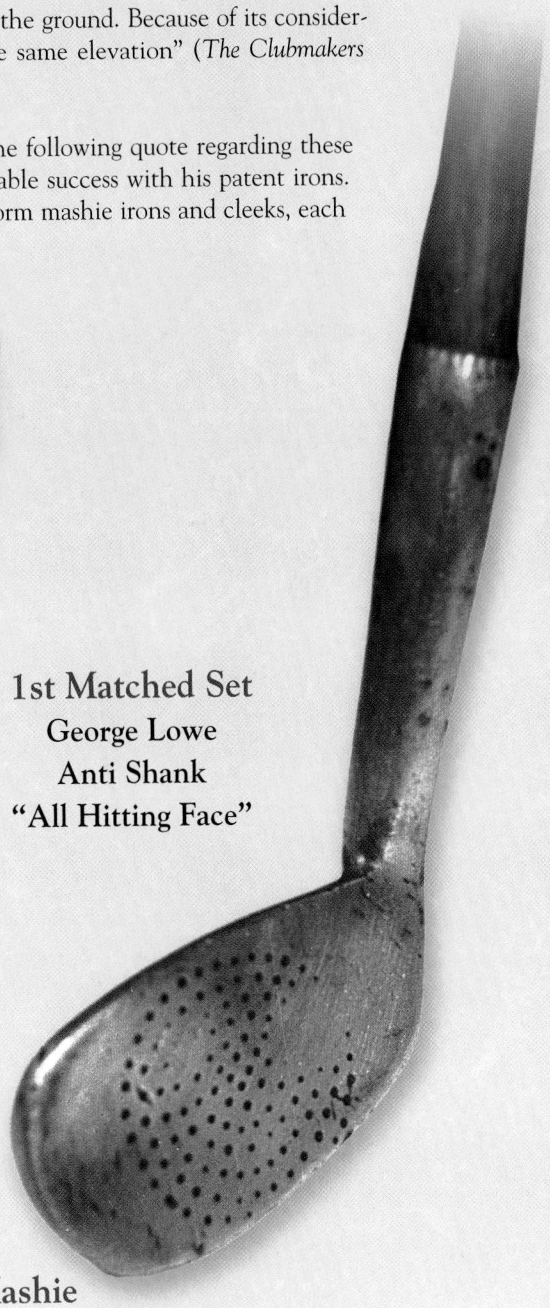

1st Matched Set
George Lowe
Anti Shank
"All Hitting Face"

Niblick

Mashie

55

HELEN HICKS FORM

Helen Hicks is convinced that women will play better golf with implements that are particularly suited to them. This chart illustrates the theory worked out for properly fitting clubs to women of various statures. It should be helpful in making the proper selection of clubs best suited to your figure and type of play. It will be to your advantage to study it carefully with an authority before making a selection.

Single Crest Identifying Symbol

Single Crest Identifying Symbol

For the small girlish figure, standing approximately five feet in height, the single crest clubs will give the best performance.

For the medium-short, moderately-stout figure, standing about five feet four inches tall, the single crest clubs will give greatest satisfaction.

PAGE 5, 1935 PROFESSIONAL

Courtesy the T.E. Wilson Company.

MATCHED CLUBS

Power and strength have little to do with a good golf shot. The perfect shot depends upon good timing and perfect rhythm. For this reason it is of prime importance that the implements for women should be finely balanced and tuned to rhythmic action. These clubs are so built, placing greater stress on swinging balance than upon actual scale weight.

Double Crest Identifying Symbol

The player of good proportion, fairly large in frame, standing about five feet six inches high, I am confident will find that the double crest clubs fit her best.

Triple Crest Identifying Symbol

Women of tall stature, standing five feet eight inches or more, will find the triple crest clubs just to their liking.

27

Courtesy the T.E. Wilson Company.

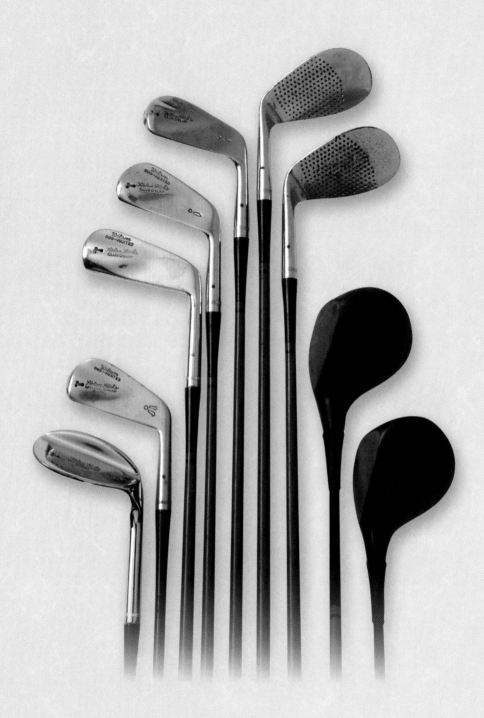

Wilson
"Helen Hicks"
"Club Champ" model
note size classification emblems on the clubs
c. 1935
short set approximate value $250.00

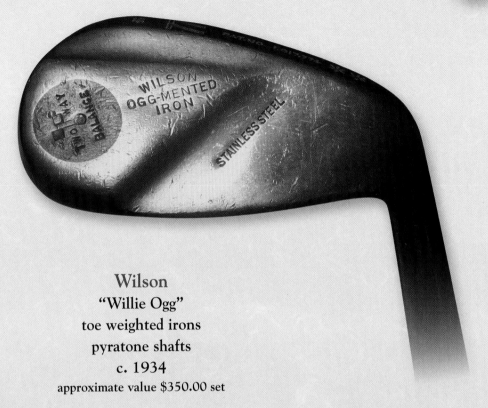

Wilson
"Willie Ogg"
toe weighted irons
pyratone shafts
c. 1934
approximate value $350.00 set

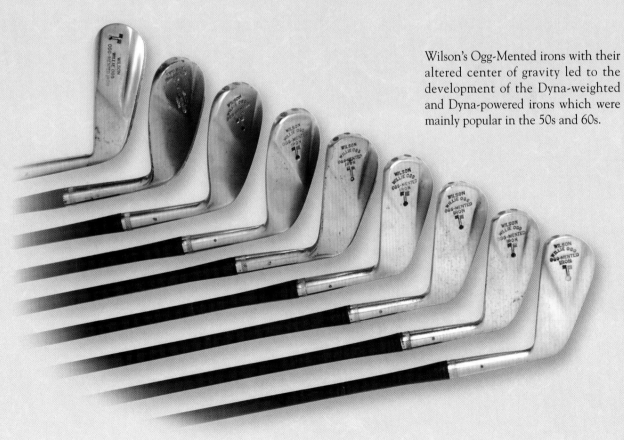

Wilson's Ogg-Mented irons with their altered center of gravity led to the development of the Dyna-weighted and Dyna-powered irons which were mainly popular in the 50s and 60s.

Wilson
"Willie Ogg"
toe weighted woods
pyratone shafts
c. 1934
approximate value $180.00 set

Lady MacGregor Stylized Clubs

To have clubs properly suited to your form and stature, you should get Lady MacGregor Stylized Clubs.

They were designed for women's play by women golfers. They are built to fit the four general types of feminine form and weight covered by the following classifications.

Because of the exactness of detail in these custom-built clubs, they are built by Gold Badge Player-Craftsmen. The specifications were determined by MacGregor research engineers through the study and measurement of three hundred average women golfers.

FOR THE TALL AND SLENDER

If you are of this type, your normal position is fairly erect. The proper clubs for you should allow you to take your natural stance comfortably without strain and distortion —so that you can make your swing freely, gracefully, and accurately. The Lady MacGregor Stylized "TS" Clubs are made especially for you.

FOR THE SHORT AND SLENDER

If you are of this type, you also normally play fairly erect; but you must have a shorter club, a shaft with more flex in it, and a grip of less diameter to accommodate your slighter wrists and smaller hands. Your requirements are met by the Lady MacGregor Stylized "PM" (Petite Miss) Clubs.

FOR THE PERFECT THIRTY-SIX

If this is your type, your most comfortable position is somewhat farther away from the ball. You need a club with a slightly heavier head and stronger shaft. Yet you cannot feel at ease with a man's club which has been shortened, for it would not be suitable for you in grip and weight and balance. Lady MacGregor "PT" Clubs are especially built for you.

FOR THE STOCKY

If this is your type, your normal stance is very flat or at a much greater angle than any of the foregoing. Your club should enable you to extend your arms comfortably when you strike the ball. The shaft must be longer and slightly stronger, the head lighter, and the club so balanced that you can swing with grace and precision. Lady MacGregor Stylized "SS" Clubs exactly meet your requirements.

YOU CAN "TRY ON" MACGREGOR CLUBS

The MacGregor dealer has a Club Selector for fitting you with clubs adapted to your personal stance and swing. When you go to the MacGregor dealer for a fitting, take along a friend whose figure is unlike yours. This will show you how the Club Selector automatically indicates the varying requirements for women of different stature.

Courtesy Crawford, MacGregor, and Canby Company.

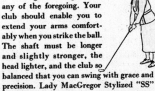

Goldsmith
putter
"Babe Didrikson"
c. 1934
approximate value $125.00

MacGregor
"Babe Didrikson"
putter
P.T. stylized classification
P.T. "Perfect Thirty-Six"
c. 1935
approximate value $125.00

Babe Didrikson
stylized P.M. (Petite Miss)
c. 1935
approximate value $75.00

Babe Didrikson
Stylized P.T. (Perfect Thirty Six)
c. 1935
approximate value $75.00

Joyce Wethered
Wethered with Babe Didrickson would likely be considered the best women golfers of all time. Bobby Jones once said of Wethered, "I have not played golf with anyone, man or woman, amateur or professional, who made me feel so utterly outclassed."

Joyce Wethered
driver & irons
c. 1928
approximate value $85.00 each

Joyce Wethered
"Running Up" iron
Gibson star in the center of the face
with "G" in the middle of the star
c. 1928
approximate value $80.00

Spalding
"Princess"
pyratone shaft
rare crown C.M.
c. 1938
approximate value $210.00 short set

A.G. Spalding & Bros.
Gold Medal
Spring Face Cleek

Made under the Cran-Cleek patent of June 1897. It was produced from 1902 to 1919. Spalding pointed to both the short hosel and the spring effect of the six riveted $\frac{1}{16}$" tempered steel face over a hollow head as significant factors in increasing driving distance.

approximate value $750.00

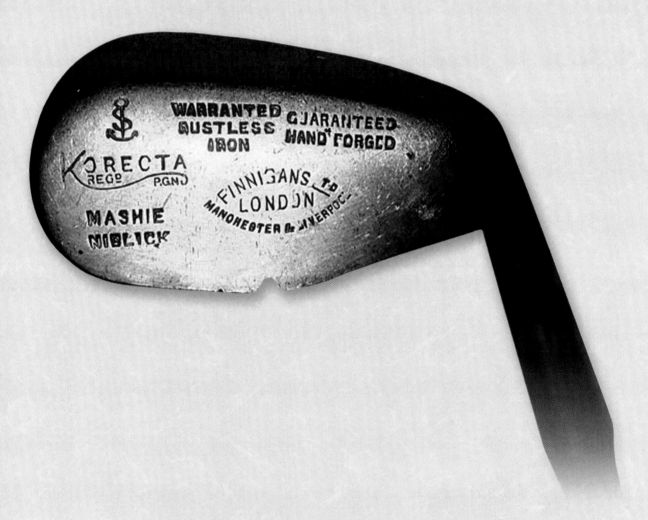

Stadium Golf Manufacturing Co. Ltd.
"Korecta" Mashie Niblick
c. 1920s
approximate value $225.00

An advanced thinking company probably most noted for producing the "PER-WHIT" putter. The sightline notch is a most uncommon feature for any iron. This club would be the equivalent of the 7 iron today.

Spalding
Michael Bingham's "Clingers"
maple leaf cleek mark
groove sole
narrow oval shaft
pyratone covered steel shaft
c. 1930
approximate value $150.00

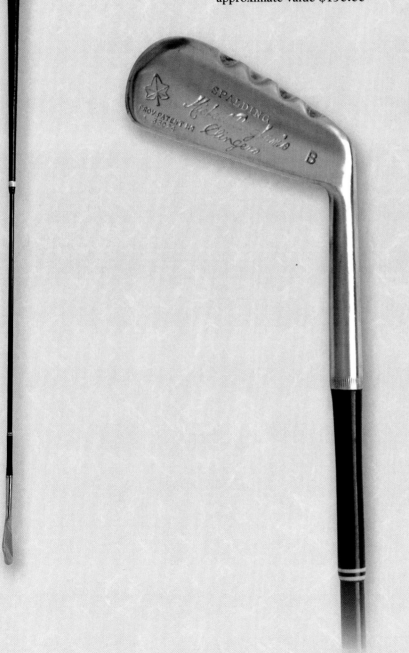

Donaldson Manufacturing Co. LTD
DRIVER-med-DURALWOOD
Rangefinder, Rapier Series, Sockethead
c. 1933
approximate value $250.00

William Hadden assigned this design to Donaldson. Not only does the featured club have this rare caped head with open bottom but this series was made with threaded hosel and shaft which allowed the user to take a shaft from one club of the set and use it in another club of the set if he desired more or less length of the club.

Wright & Ditson
slit hosel
c. 1930s
approximate value $75.00 single club
approximate value $450.00 short set

Walter Hagen
"Tomboy"
c. 1933
note similarity of the wood club
heads to Lucky Len putter
approximate value $450.00 short set

Unknown maker
"ParMetl" spoon
A rare club with a face plate insert of a hard fiber-like material held by
three brass plugs. Metal shafted with weight placed at the rear from
the top edge to the center of the club or sweet spot. This hollow-
backed club with this innovation should have an interesting ball flight.
c. 1920s
approximate value $250.00

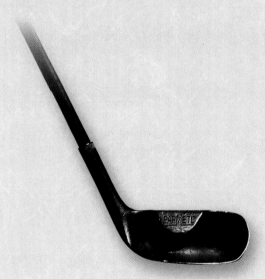

Wilson
"Walker Cup"
pyratone shaft
single club approximate value $36.00
short set approximate value $210.00

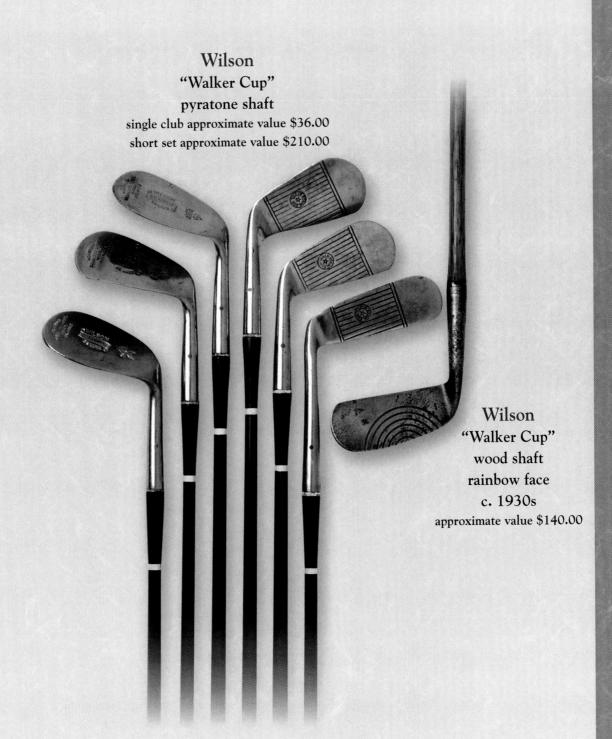

Wilson
"Walker Cup"
wood shaft
rainbow face
c. 1930s
approximate value $140.00

BTN - Butchart - Nicholls Co.
wood center
circular core surrounded by six
lenghts of bamboo
c. 1930
approximate value $2,050.00

Spalding
"Linerite"
pyratone shaft
rare use of "Bobby Jones" as the signature
A green line runs down the shaft to show the player how to line up his shot.
c. 1938
approximate value $65.00 each
short set with putter approximate value $650.00

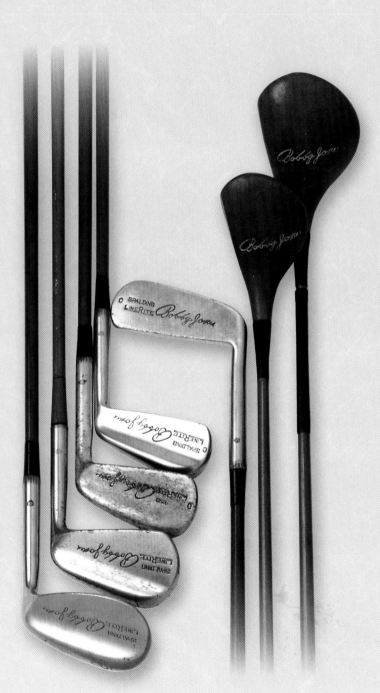

Banner
wood shaft
A store line for Kroydon. The first four
clubs have horizontal lines but the niblick,
in a rare departure, is vertically lined.
c. 1920s
horizontal line clubs
approximate value $135.00 each
50 degree vertical line niblick
approximate value $350.00 each

MacGregor
3852 Series
Tommy Armour signature
TA Ironmaster
putter & wedge
c. 1938
approximate value $675.00 full set

Reading from left to right: BOBBY JONES and the Spalding Clubs he designed

Hᴇʀᴇ is Bobby Jones examining the first set of golf clubs ever made which offer his idea of what perfect golf clubs should be!

From 8 to 1, is a set of the grandest Irons that the game has ever seen. Jones, now a Spalding Director, and the Spalding experts have, by redistributing weight, succeeded in designing an iron whose head tends to follow through naturally. As Jones himself expressed it, "the blade seems to flow through the ball."

This redistribution of weight—the heavier blade and lighter hosel—gives better control, too. The center of percussion is two inches lower than it is on hickory-shafted irons, and an inch lower than it is on other steel-shafted irons. This makes the clubhead easier to direct, and gives a more perfect instrument for shot control.

Another factor which contributes to control is the flange sole, which seats itself in back of the ball with the accuracy of a putter. This feature relieves the player of the distracting business of fussing with the lie of the blade, and lets him concentrate on the stroke itself.

In these clubs, Jones also cuts the number of stances right in half, by introducing the brand new idea of matching in pairs as to length and lie! This means that you need master only *one* stance for every *two* clubs. And, every club is matched with every other club in swinging weight—so that one swing and one timing are correct for every club in the set!

"Poems in Wood"

Bobby Jones is recognized as one of the greatest wood players of all time. And his uncanny skill is reflected in the new woods which he designed. One famous expert, when first examining them, said—"They're poems in wood." When perfectly sane golfers get to talking like that about these clubs, they *must* be magnificent!

In addition to the customary woods, Jones contributes a new Senior Set of *Five* Graduated Woods—introducing two completely new woods to take the place of the Numbers 1 and 2 irons. Senior golfers will find, in this Set, a solution of the difficulties they now have with their long iron shots.

Look! It's Calamity Jane!

That interesting looking club on the end is none other than Calamity Jane—an exact duplicate of the famous lady herself. Legend has it that Bobby Jones clings to this great putter because he considers it "lucky." In a way, that's true. Calamity Jane's magnificent balance and deadliness make it a lucky club in any golfer's bag.

Lower prices for all

The new Jones Clubs have the famous Spalding Cushion-neck. The sets are Registered, so that you can always get an exact duplicate of any club. And the prices are the lowest ever asked for Spalding fine clubs.

CUSTOM-BUILT REGISTERED IRONS
Set of 9 $75   Set of 8 $67   Set of 6 $50
(Cushion Shaft Irons, $5 each)

CUSTOM-BUILT DE LUXE REGISTERED WOODS
Set of 4 $48   Set of 3 $36   Pair $24

CUSTOM-BUILT STANDARD REGISTERED WOODS
Set of 4 $40   Set of 3 $30   Pair $20
(Autograph Woods, separately, $8 and $10 each)

Custom-Built De Luxe Senior Graduated Registered Woods, $60 for set of 5. Senior Graduated Matched Woods, $40 for set of 5. Calamity Jane Putter, $6.

Spalding
ROBERT T. JONES, JR.
GOLF CLUBS

Spalding
pyratone shaft
full set with utitlity iron and P.D.N. wedge
cushion neck registered matching Kro-Flite woods
with Calamity Jane putter
c. 1932
approximate value $500.00

Spalding
changes in shaft and ferrule
color – design changes
c. 1932 – 1941

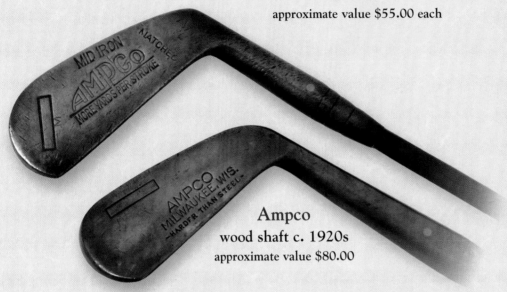

Ampco
made of a special metal harder than steel
claimed to hit the ball farther
c. 1919
approximate value $55.00 each

Ampco
wood shaft c. 1920s
approximate value $80.00

Assorted Scottish makers
c. 1930
approximate value
$30.00 each

J. Aitken
head pro, Wentworth
"No Shok" rustless
c. 1932
approximate value
$200.00 short set

Beckley-Ralston
From left to right:
Walloper, steel shaft, c. 1927, approximate value $40.00
Chipper, steel shaft, c. 1930s, approximate value $40.00
Chipper, "Shotmaker," wood shaft, c. 1930s, approximate value $135.00
Putter, "Shotmaker," pencil shaft, c. 1930s, approximate value $55.00

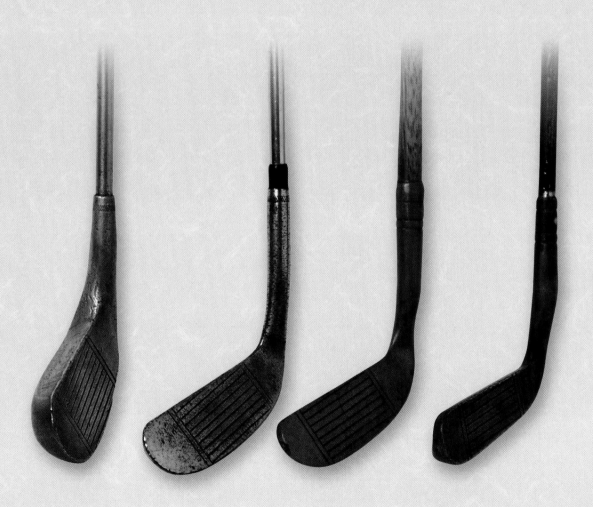

George Nicholls
"Rustless"
iron set with putter
pyratone shaft
c. 1930s
approximate value $250.00 set

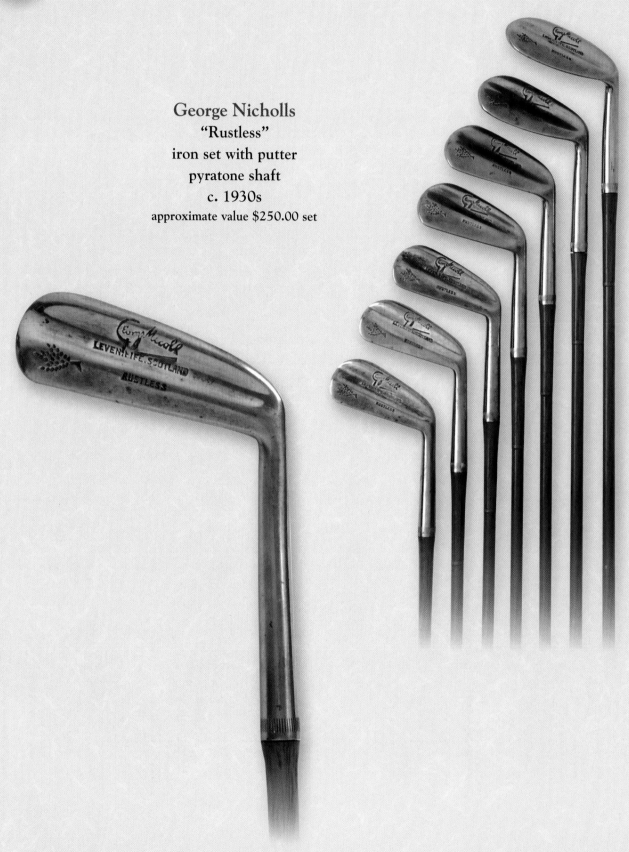

Burr-Key Bilt
"Classic Series"
wood, pyratone, and steel shafted
brass disc insert in the face
c. 1920s
approximate value $135.00 each

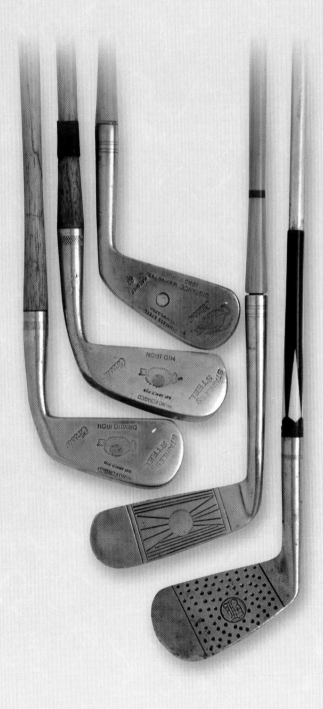

W. Hagen
spiral shaft
c. 1930s
approximate value
$1,200.00 set

Wright & Ditson
"Harry Cooper"
pyratone shaft
c. 1931
approximate value $250.00 set

A five-time Open winner Taylor with Braid and Vardon made up "golf's great triumvirate," a triad that dominated British golf at the turn of the century.

J. H. Taylor
"personal model"
pyratone shaft
c. 1938
approximate value $350.00 set,
including putter

Unknown maker
all wood set
laminated heads with loft corresponding to the
iron of the same number
c. 1940s
approximate value $800.00

putter

2 iron

3 iron

5 iron

7 iron

8 iron

9 iron

3 wood

2 wood

driver

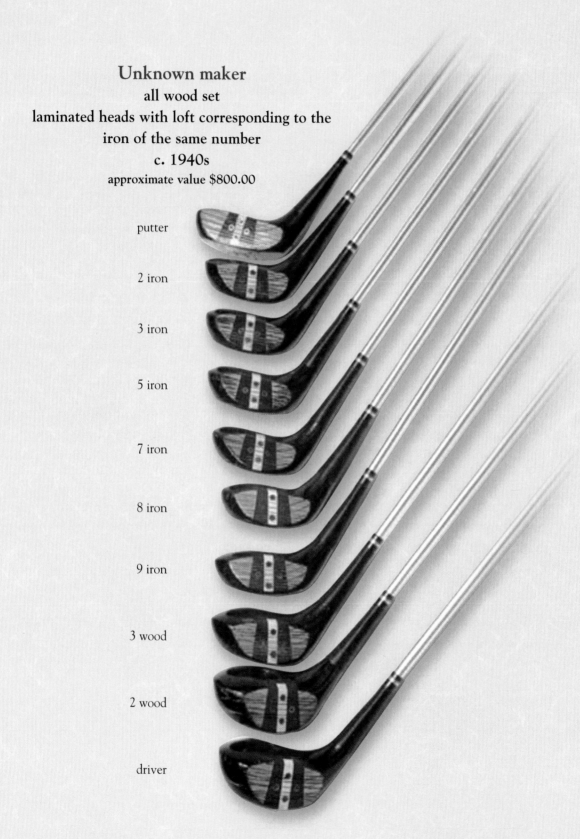

Composite Materials

R Forgan
The "Tolley" putter
named for amateur champion Cyril Tolley
made of a composite material called Forganite
c. 1927
approximate value $350.00

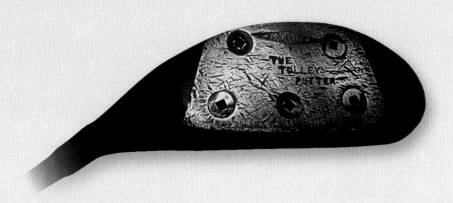

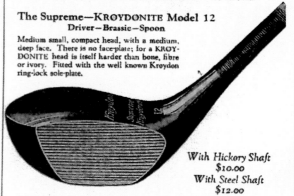

KROYDONITE
The World's Hardest Hitting Clubs

MOST IMPORTANT of many Kroydon improvements in wood clubs is KROYDONITE which renders wood heads absolutely moisture proof, and at the same time so *dense* and *flinty-hard* that they give many yards of *added distance.*

KROYDONITE is a newly developed chemical. In a molten state, and under great pressure, it is forced into every pore and fibre of the wood.

When dry, these wood heads are as *dense* and *hard* as metal. They will never contract or expand through absorption of moisture—and *their parts will not work loose.*

KROYDONITE clubs are made in 3 models—$7 to $12.

The Supreme—KROYDONITE Model 12
Driver—Brassie—Spoon

Medium small, compact head, with a medium, deep face. There is no face-plate; for a KROYDONITE head is itself harder than bone, fibre or ivory. Fitted with the well known Kroydon ring-lock sole-plate.

With *Hickory Shaft*
$10.00
With *Steel Shaft*
$12.00

Kroydon ad

Kroydon
"Kroydonite"
c. 1930s
approximate value $75.00

Hard Wright
"Condensite"
aluminum ferrule
c. 1917
approximate value $575.00

Unknown maker
curved steel shaft
"St. Andrews Bend."
The only identification I have on
this club is PAT.389 on the sole.
Dimensions are 5' in lengh by
1⅜" deep with 1" face made of
a material like forganite or
ebonite but appears more fragile.
c. 1930s
approximate value $750.00
actual size

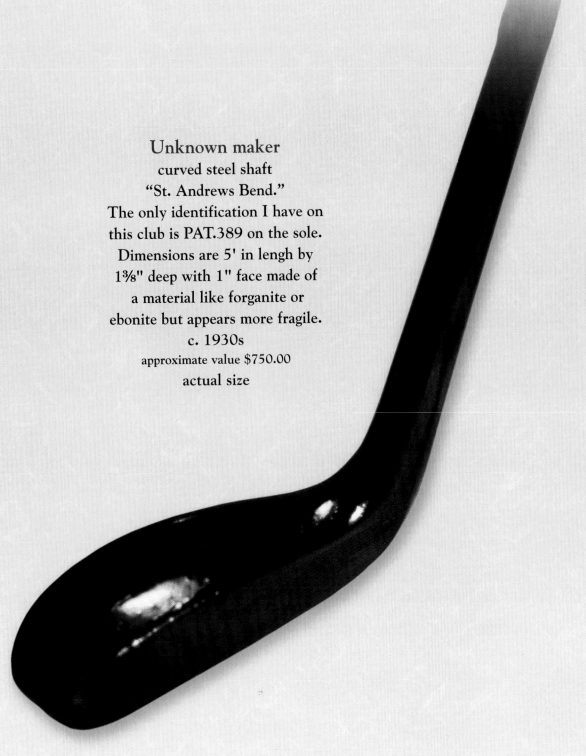

Textolite
a composite material molded by
General Electric for Schavolite Golf
c. 1934
approximate value $55.00 each
approximate value $275.00 set

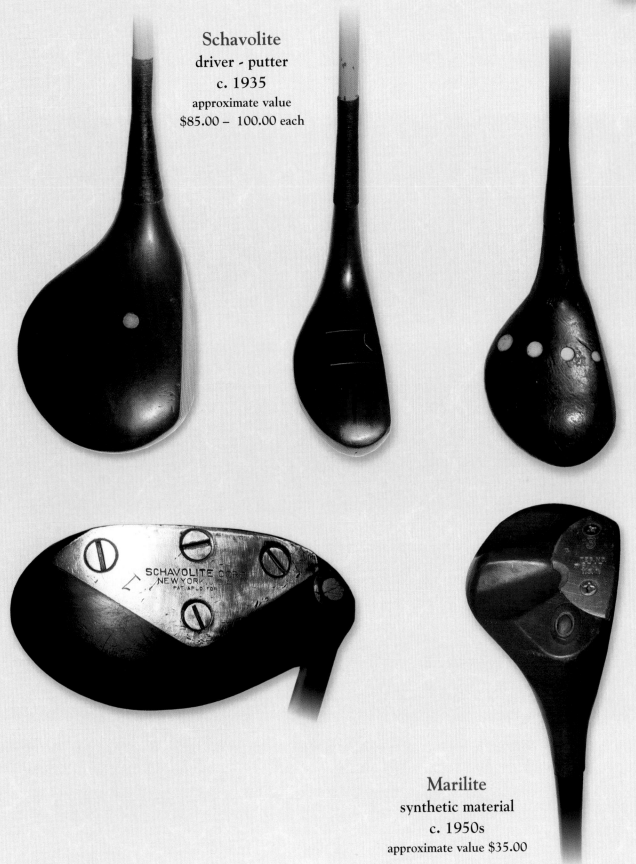

Schavolite
driver - putter
c. 1935
approximate value
$85.00 – 100.00 each

SCHAVOLITE CORP
NEW YORK
PAT. APLD FOR

Marilite
synthetic material
c. 1950s
approximate value $35.00

Stan Thompson
driver - "Whistler"
hard plastic
slotted head
Thompson, a very innovative designer,
was best known for the Ginty Series.
c. 1950s
approximate value $300.00

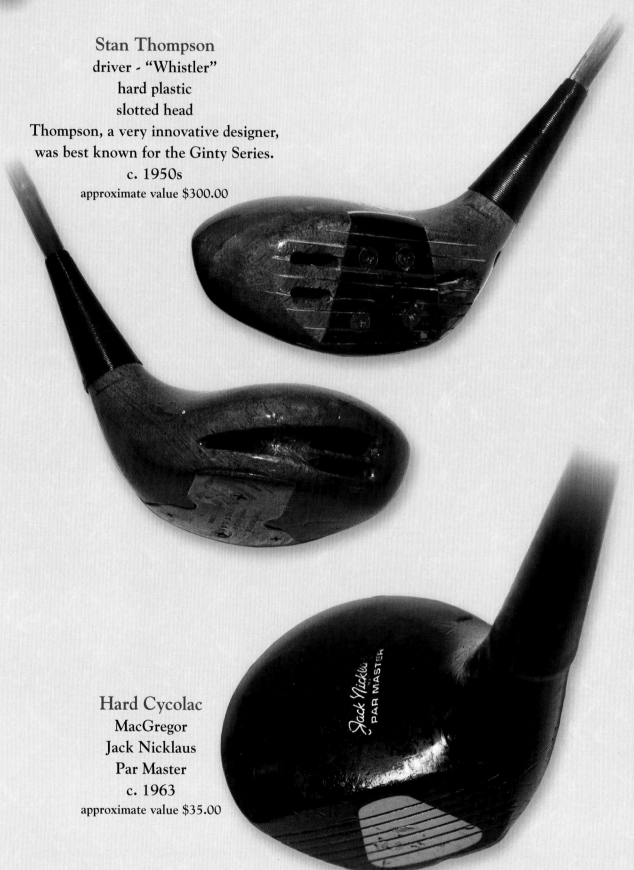

Hard Cycolac
MacGregor
Jack Nicklaus
Par Master
c. 1963
approximate value $35.00

Unknown maker
"The Pre O"
Synthetic material with brass
covering the putting area on
both sides. One of the most
unusual, but with great
putting capability.
c. 1960
approximate value $130.00

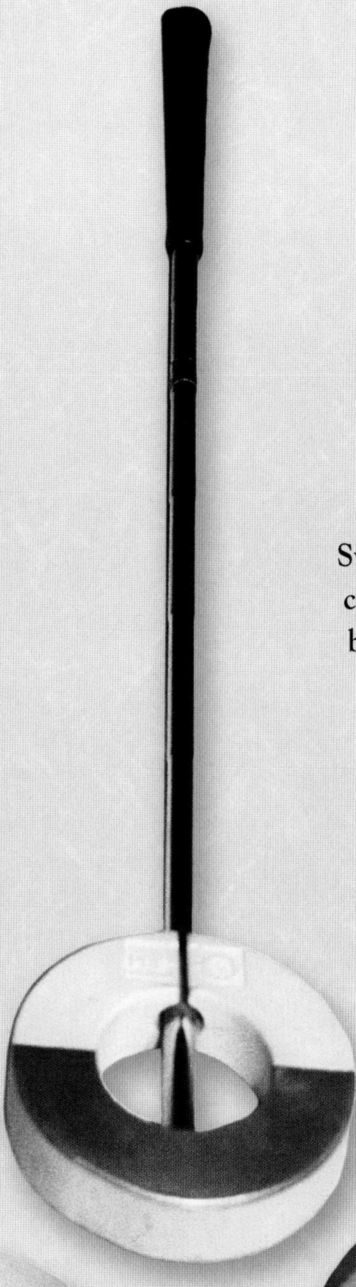

Spalding
"Cran Cleek"
pyratone shaft
synthetic insert
Chick Fraser was a club pro in southern California in the early 1920s.
Originally patented in 1897, they were last offered with wood shafts and wood inserts.
The "Fraser" pictured is rarer than all others.
approximate value $800.00

Fancy Face Woods

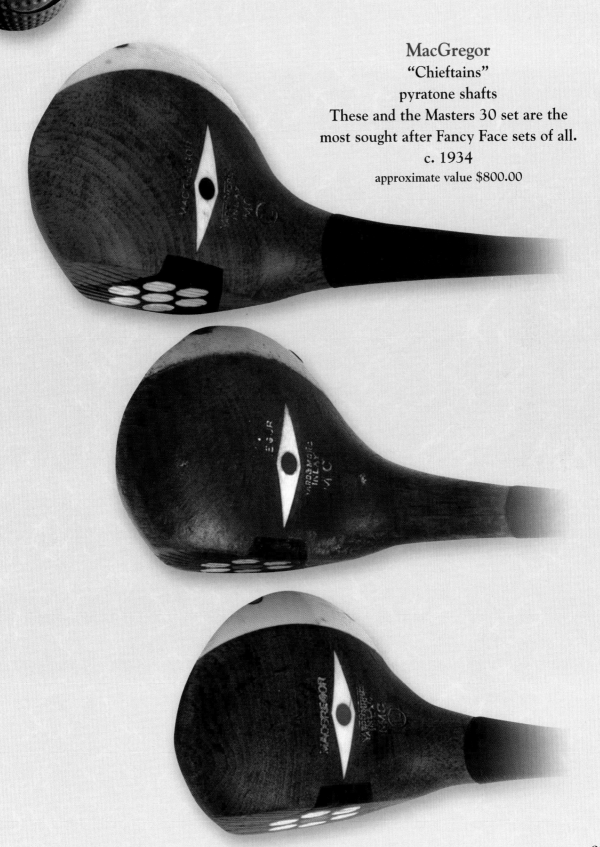

MacGregor
"Chieftains"
pyratone shafts
These and the Masters 30 set are the
most sought after Fancy Face sets of all.
c. 1934
approximate value $800.00

MacGregor
steel shaft
Different color dots indicate
the number of the wood.
red – driver – 1 wood
green – Brassie – 2 wood
gold – spoon – 3 wood
c. 1929
approximate value $425.00

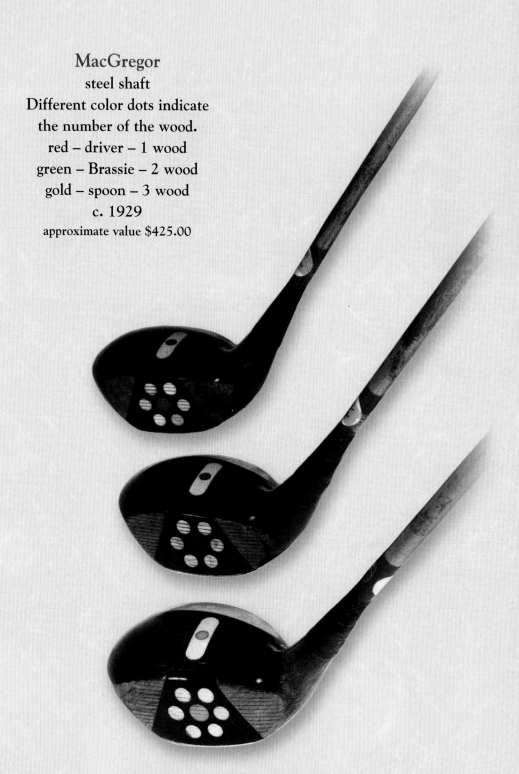

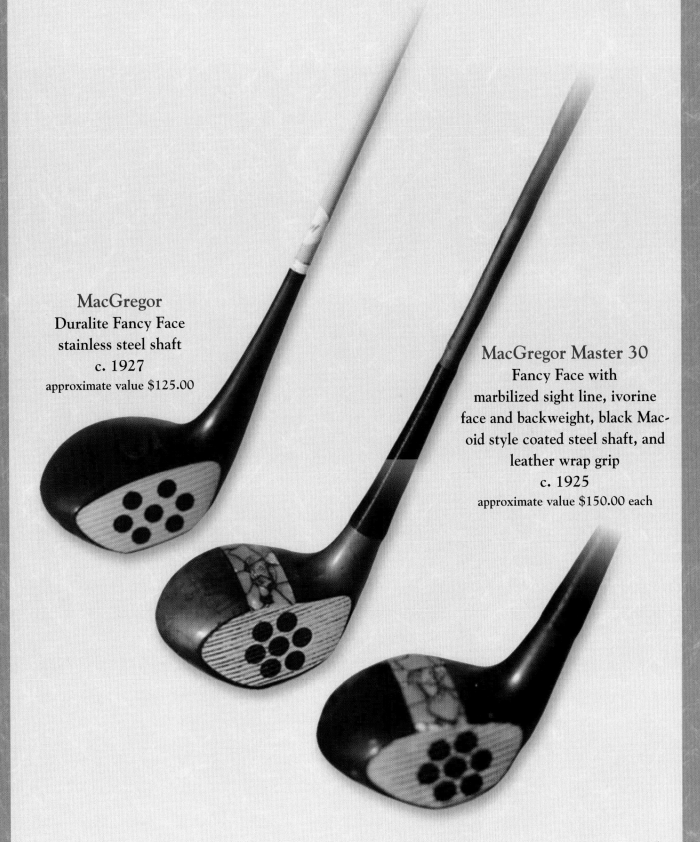

MacGregor
Duralite Fancy Face
stainless steel shaft
c. 1927
approximate value $125.00

MacGregor Master 30
Fancy Face with
marbilized sight line, ivorine
face and backweight, black Mac-
oid style coated steel shaft, and
leather wrap grip
c. 1925
approximate value $150.00 each

Custom Bilt
Fancy Face 3 wood
mother of pearl insert
grip cap of likely Bakelite with green
dot indicating 3 wood
ivory backweight with green dot
c. 1930s
approximate value $120.00 each

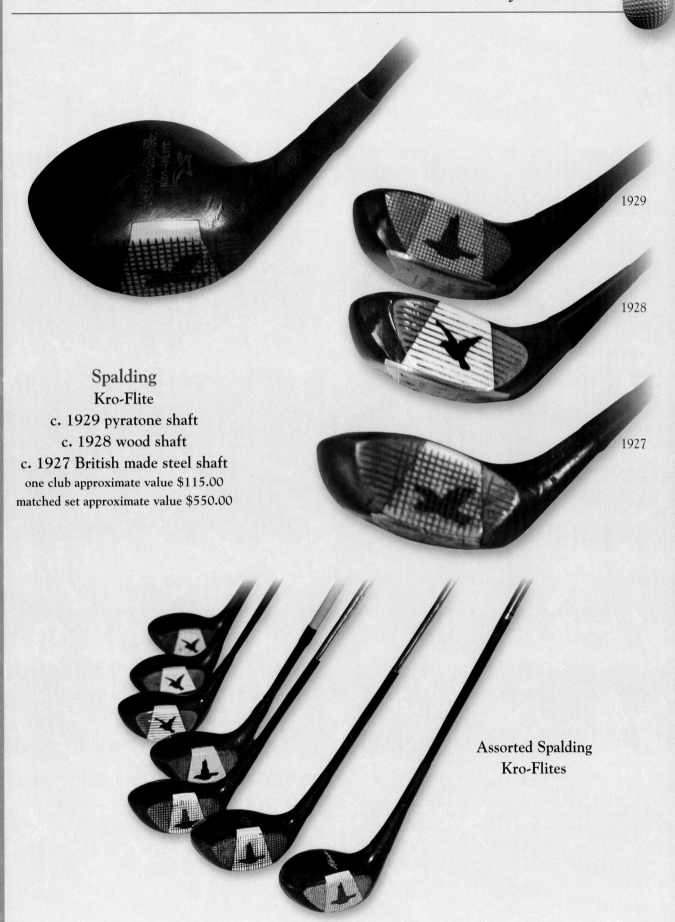

1929

1928

1927

Spalding
Kro-Flite
c. 1929 pyratone shaft
c. 1928 wood shaft
c. 1927 British made steel shaft
one club approximate value $115.00
matched set approximate value $550.00

**Assorted Spalding
Kro-Flites**

SPALDING

QUALITY

**Model P
PRESENTATION
Top and Side
Views**

**Model 1015
REGISTERED
Top and Side
Views**

**Model 1000
REGISTERED
Top and Side
Views**

**LITTLE
SLAMMER
SPOON
Top and Side
Views**

**Model K1000
AUTOGRAPH
Top and Side
Views**

SPALDING
STEEL-SHAFTED WOOD CLUBS

PRESENTATION CLUB. Driver, Brassie or Spoon.
Model P. True Temper Steel Shaft. Chromium finished. Fibreloid binding. The face of this club carries any one initial, on special order. Can also be supplied with a Pyratone Sleeve when specified. An ideal prize for tournament play. . . . . Each, **$25.00**

REGISTERED KRO-FLITE. Driver, Brassie or Spoon.
Supplied in shafts as noted.
Men's right hand—
Model 1000. True Temper Steel Shaft, Pyratone Sleeve.
Model 1015. True Temper Steel Shaft, Chromium plated. Cushion neck. Fibreloid binding. Model 2000. Bristol Steel Shaft, Chromium plated, with cushion neck.
Men's left hand—
Model 1000. True Temper Steel Shaft, Pyratone Sleeve.
Model 1015. True Temper Steel Shaft. Chromium plated. Cushion neck. Fibreloid binding. Model 2000. Bristol Steel Shaft. Chromium plated, with cushion neck.
Women's right hand only—
Model 1010W. True Temper Steel Shaft. Chromium plated, with cushion neck.
Pair, **$30.00**   Set of 3, **$45.00**

LITTLE SLAMMER SPOON—REGISTERED.
Model K100. Men's right hand only. Supplied in True Temper Steel Shaft. Chromium plated, with cushion neck. . . . . Each, **$15.00**

AUTOGRAPH K. Driver, Brassie or Spoon.
Supplied in shafts as noted.
Men's right hand—
Model K54D. Bristol Steel Shaft, chromium plated, fibreloid binding. Cushion neck.
Model K965. True Temper Steel Shaft, with Pyratone Sleeve.
Model K1000. True Temper Steel Shaft, chromium plated, fibreloid binding. Cushion neck.
Men's left hand—
Model K54D. Bristol Steel Shaft. Chromium plated, fibreloid binding. Cushion neck.
Women's right hand only:
Model K1010W. True Temper Steel Shaft, chromium plated. Cushion neck.
Models K965 and K1000. ¾ Duralumin sole plate, lead back.
Model K54D. Duncan patented combination weight and sole plate. Maltese cross face; Black face Driver; Red face Brassie; White face Spoon. Stain, mahogany, with one-half inch natural stripe. . . . . Each, **$12.50**

ALL PRICES SUBJECT TO CHANGE WITHOUT NOTICE. ALL ORDERS WILL BE ACCEPTED SUBJECT ONLY TO OUR ABILITY TO SUPPLY THE GOODS. PRICES SHOWN ARE THOSE IN EFFECT ON DATE NOTED BELOW.

PAGE 38—JANUARY 5, 1929

Spalding Catalog, p. 38, January 1929.

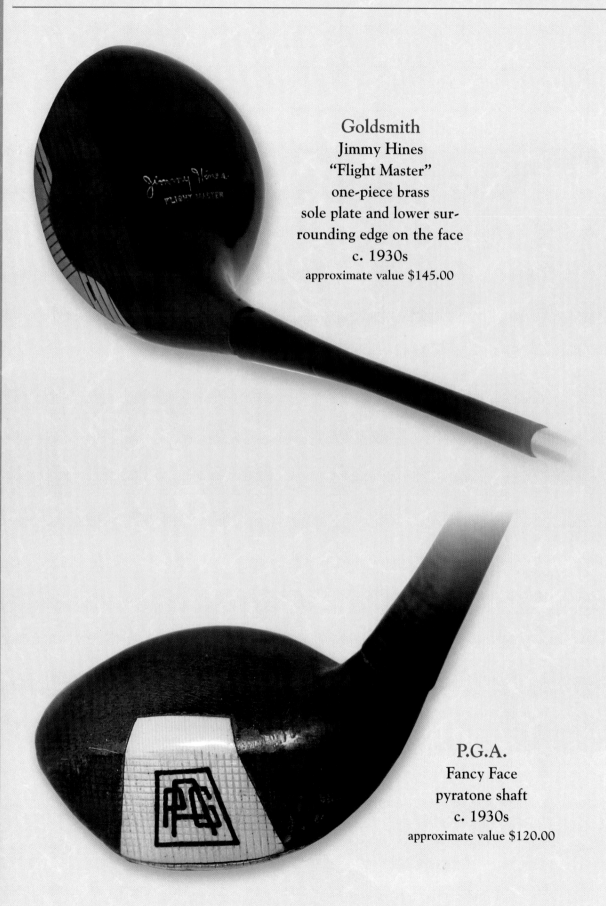

Goldsmith
Jimmy Hines
"Flight Master"
one-piece brass
sole plate and lower sur-
rounding edge on the face
c. 1930s
approximate value $145.00

P.G.A.
Fancy Face
pyratone shaft
c. 1930s
approximate value $120.00

Burke
Fancy Face driver
c. 1927
approximate value $120.00

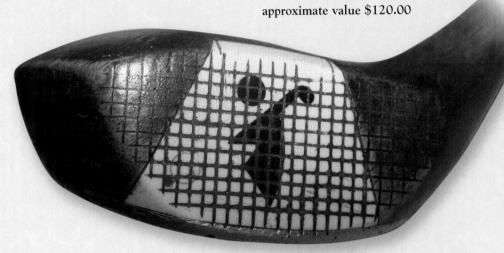

Allied
the "Whippet" Fancy Face
whippet or greyhound emblem
pyratone shaft
c. 1930s
approximate value $165.00

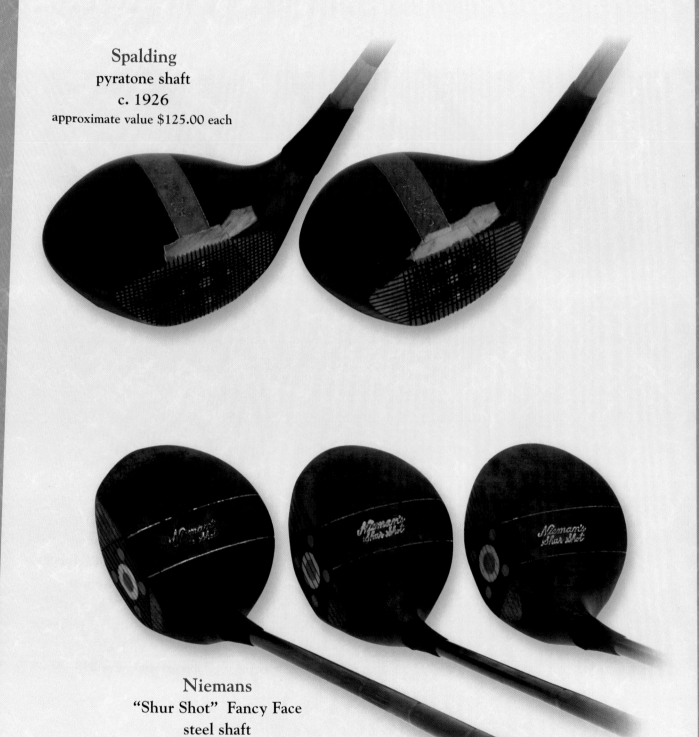

Spalding
pyratone shaft
c. 1926
approximate value $125.00 each

Niemans
"Shur Shot" Fancy Face
steel shaft
c. 1930s
approximate value $245.00

Billings
matched set
chromium covered
steel shafts
c. 1938
approximate value $250.00 set

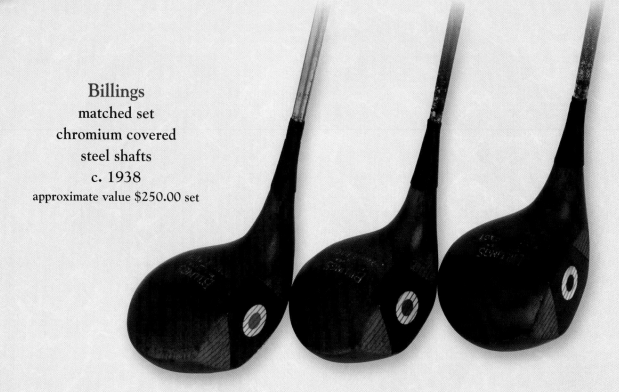

Vulcan
"V-44" patent pending
pyratone shaft
c. 1930
approximate value $250.00

Spalding
pyratone shaft
c. 1926
approximate value $125.00 each

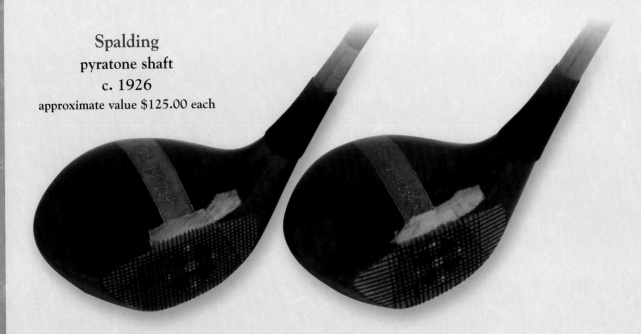

Niemans
"Shur Shot" Fancy Face
steel shaft
c. 1930s
approximate value $245.00

Burr-Key Bilt
"Regal"
black metal shaft
c. 1930s
approximate value $75.00 each

Spalding Fancy Face
c. 1926
approximate value
$70.00 each

MacGregor
Fancy Face
Top: "Go Sum" driver,
No. 50 spoon
Bottom: "Go Sum"
brassie, No. 50 brassie
c. 1920s
approximate value $95.00 each

Assorted Fancy Face clubs
in good or better condition, G-7 – G-8
approximate value $70.00 each

Assorted Fancy Face clubs
pyratone, Mac-oid, painted, or
chrome shafts
c. 1923 – 1940
approximate value $70.00 each

Assorted Fancy Face clubs
pyratone, Mac-oid, painted, or
chrome shafts
c. 1923 – 1940
approximate value $70.00 each

Assorted Fancy Face clubs
pyratone, Mac-oid, painted, or
chrome shafts
c. 1923 – 1940
approximate value $70.00 each

Assorted Fancy Face clubs
pyratone, Mac-oid, painted, or
chrome shafts
c. 1923 – 1940
approximate value $70.00 each

Wright & Ditson
"Record" Fancy Face
c. 1926
approximate value $85.00 each

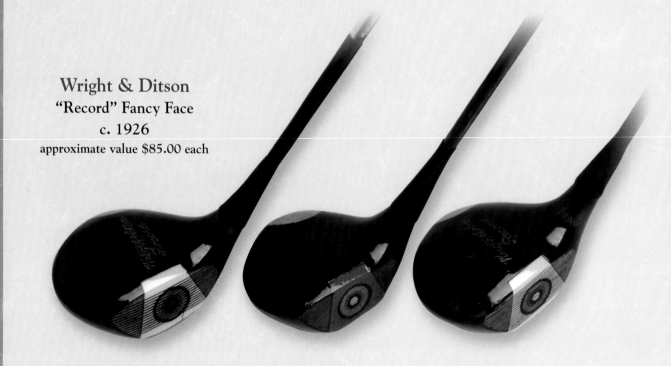

W. Hagan
Fancy Face
1 - "Fairway"
2 - "Braeburn"
3 - "W. H. C."
c. 1930
approximate value $85.00 each

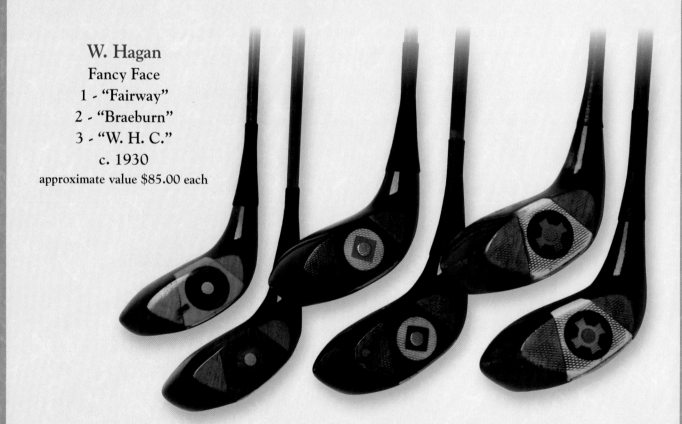

Burke Co.
Lady Burke
brassie & driver
c. 1927
approximate value $70.00 each

Burke Co.
"Aristo" deluxe model
black steel shaft
c. 1933
approximate value $85.00 each

Walter Hagen
"Fairway" driver
black pyratone shaft
c. 1936
approximate value $140.00

Walter Hagen
Fancy Face
single piece sole &
insert of brass
c. 1930s
approximate value
$200.00 set

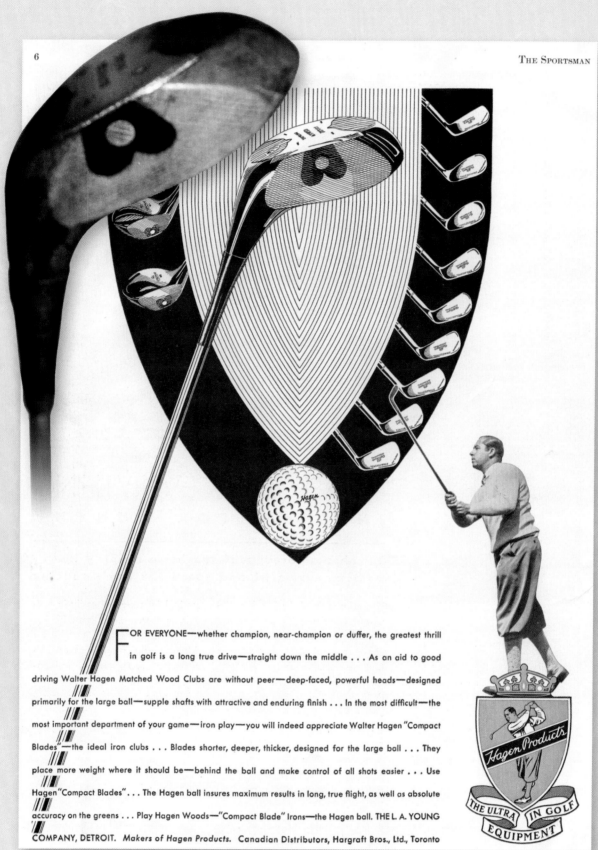

6   THE SPORTSMAN

FOR EVERYONE—whether champion, near-champion or duffer, the greatest thrill in golf is a long true drive—straight down the middle . . . As an aid to good driving Walter Hagen Matched Wood Clubs are without peer—deep-faced, powerful heads—designed primarily for the large ball—supple shafts with attractive and enduring finish . . . In the most difficult—the most important department of your game—iron play—you will indeed appreciate Walter Hagen "Compact Blades"—the ideal iron clubs . . . Blades shorter, deeper, thicker, designed for the large ball . . . They place more weight where it should be—behind the ball and make control of all shots easier . . . Use Hagen "Compact Blades" . . . The Hagen ball insures maximum results in long, true flight, as well as absolute accuracy on the greens . . . Play Hagen Woods—"Compact Blade" Irons—the Hagen ball. THE L. A. YOUNG COMPANY, DETROIT. *Makers of Hagen Products.* Canadian Distributors, Hargraft Bros., Ltd., Toronto

Courtesy Hagen Products and the L.A. Young Company.

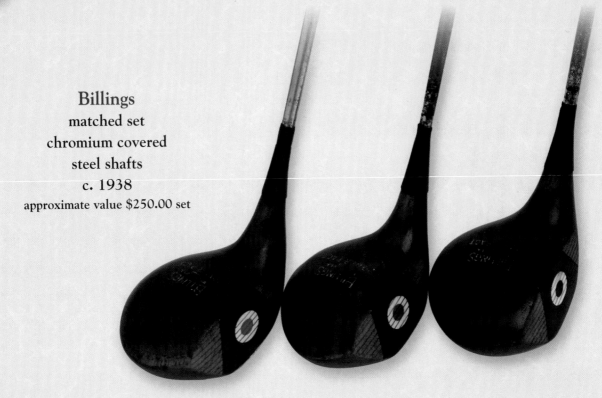

Billings
matched set
chromium covered
steel shafts
c. 1938
approximate value $250.00 set

Vulcan
"V-44" patent pending
pyratone shaft
c. 1930
approximate value $250.00

Kroydon
1 wood shaft, c. 1923
2 steel shaft, c. 1930s
3 pyratone shaft, c. 1930s
approximate value
$200.00 each

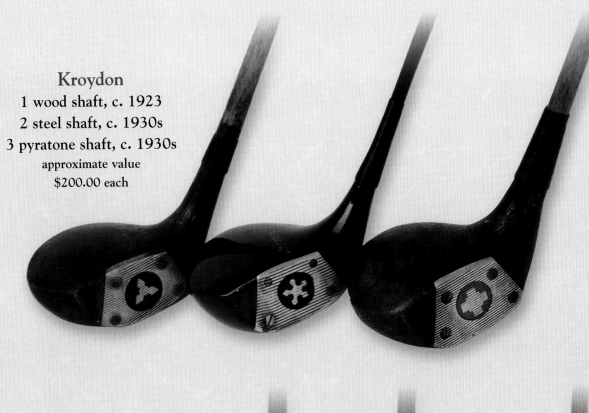

MacGregor
"Yards More Inlay"
matched set
pyratone shaft
c. 1923
approximate value $325.00 set

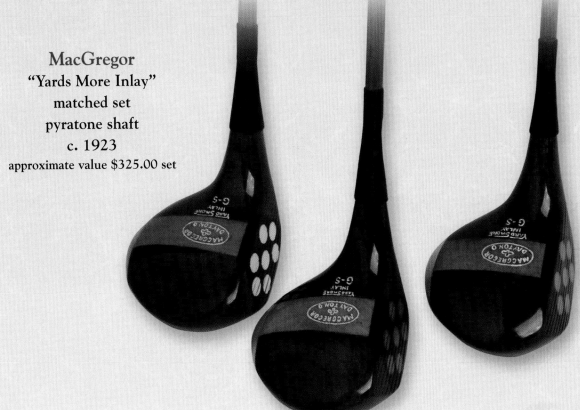

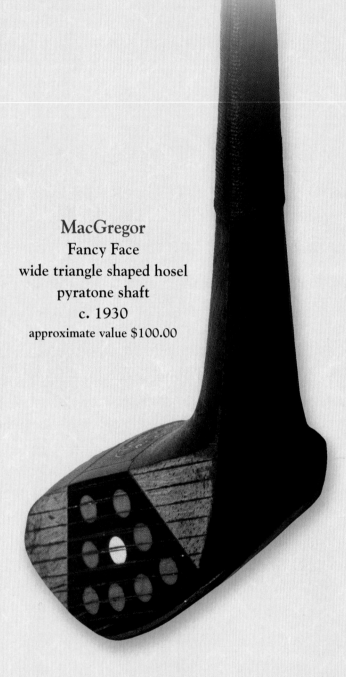

MacGregor
Fancy Face
wide triangle shaped hosel
pyratone shaft
c. 1930
approximate value $100.00

Walter Hagen
Fancy Face driver
with one-piece head and
6" hosel
whipping left off to show
the joining of hosel &
pyratone shaft
c. 1928
approximate value $85.00

Spalding
Robert Jones Jr.
"Deluxe Registered" model
pyratone shaft
c. 1934
approximate value $80.00 each
approximate value $300.00 set

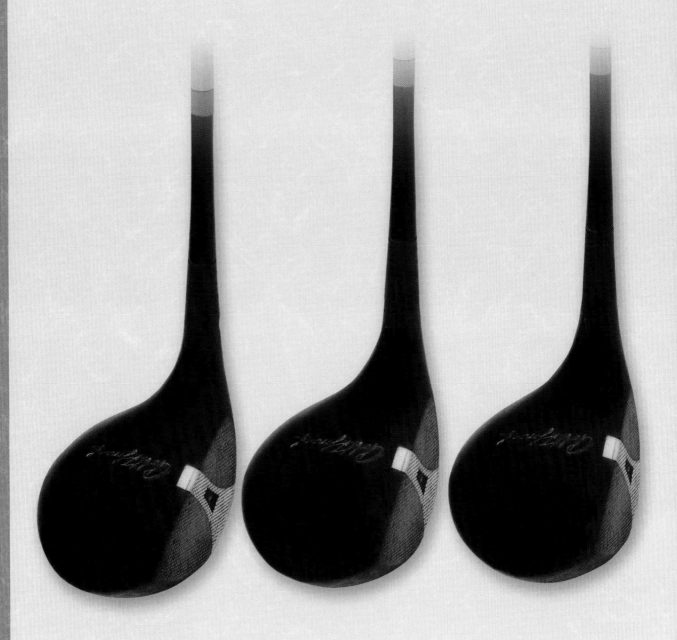

Wilson
"Ryder Cup"
pyratone shaft
c. 1927
approximate value $110.00 each
three club matched set approximate value $410.00

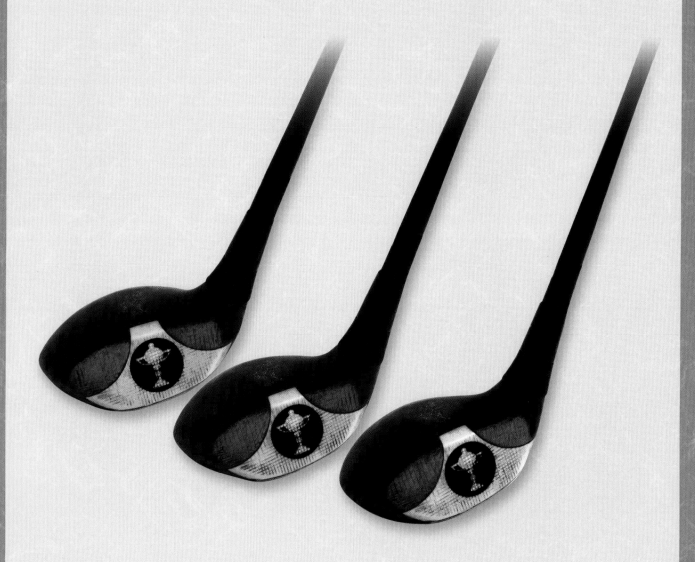

Wilson
"Walker Cup" Fancy Face
pyratone shaft
c. 1927
approximate value $410.00 set

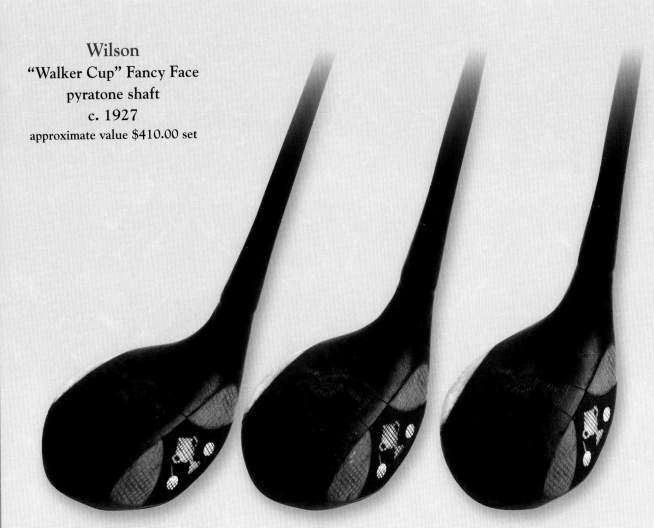

Fancy Face Putters & Irons

MacGregor
"Ivora" putter
Sweet spot alignment aid
c. 1915
approximate value $285.00

Dedstop Irons
Manufactured with holes in the face, brick patterns, deep slots, various shaped grooves, waffle, rainbow, and other patterns. Used in 1914 – 1921 but banned after the Jock Hutchison win of the 1921 Open. The Royal & Ancient felt this win was mainly due to their use. The U.S.G.A. concurred and banned them effective 1924.
approximate value $160.00 each

Mac & Mac
deep dimple face
This club was intended to replace
those "Dedstop" or deep grooved
clubs banned by the R & A. It,
too, was banned in 1924.
c. 1923
approximate value $500.00

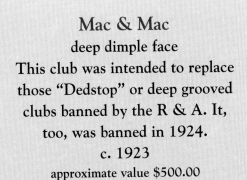

Banner
Brick face
c. 1920s
approximate value $350.00

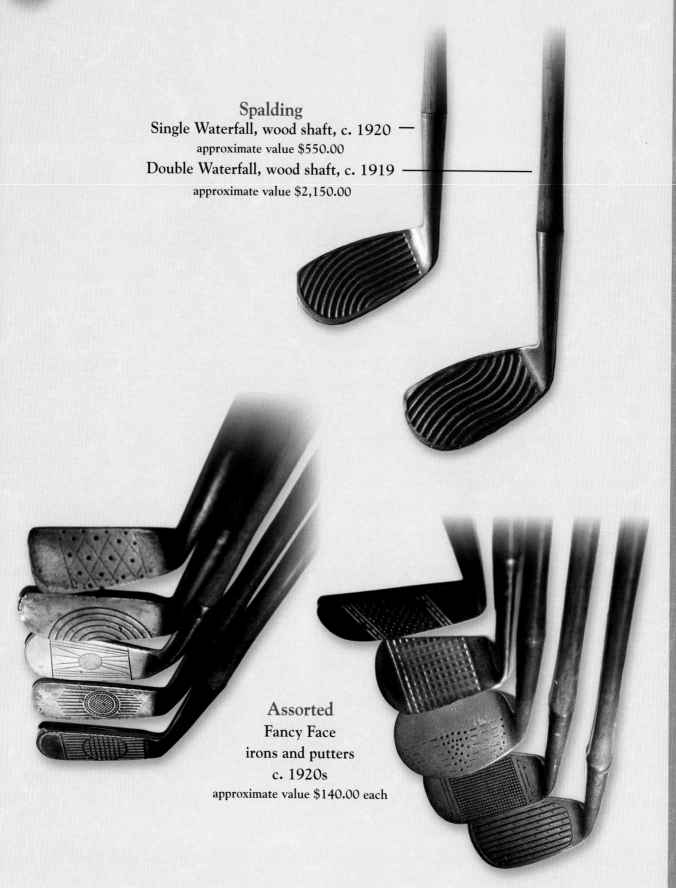

Spalding
Single Waterfall, wood shaft, c. 1920 —
approximate value $550.00
Double Waterfall, wood shaft, c. 1919 ———
approximate value $2,150.00

Assorted
Fancy Face
irons and putters
c. 1920s
approximate value $140.00 each

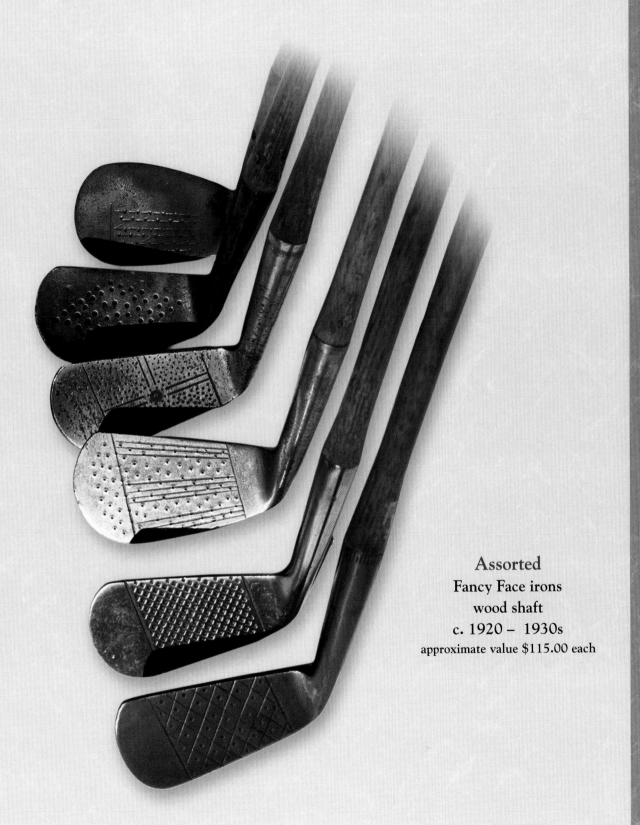

Assorted
Fancy Face irons
wood shaft
c. 1920 – 1930s
approximate value $115.00 each

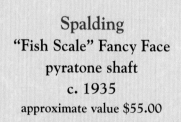

Spalding
"Fish Scale" Fancy Face
pyratone shaft
c. 1935
approximate value $55.00

DESIGN PATENT
APPLIED FOR

First Flight
"Ripple" face
pyratone shaft
c. 1937
approximate value $55.00

Alex Taylor
"Niblick"
"Honeycomb" Fancy Face
pyratone shaft
c. 1934
approximate value $95.00

Utility Irons

Similiary of Club Design

At least two to five years before the invention of the sand wedge in 1932, the Skoogee wedge and other less known niblicks came into existence and were played by many. They are remarkably close in form and function to the 1932 sand wedge. To me, a club must have a distinctly unusual shape or function to warrant authorship. Having said that, I am well aware of the concept of and conflict which results from "spontaneous invention." A happening, not uncommon when a narrow subject such as golf club shape, and utitlity is being continually investigated and improved. Almost identical ideas or products have occurred simultaneously even when developed in the most secret laboratories or by individuals, thousands of miles apart, or where there was no possibility of shared information. Dozens of clubs created now have look-alike cousins of 50 years or more ago. Few are truly inventions. Many are not improvements. The bounce soled wedges, with a change in the angle of the sole facilitating the exit of the head from the sand, were introduced by Wilson in 1932.

Gibson & Co.
The "Skoogee" niblick
concave face
c. 1930
approximate value $450.00

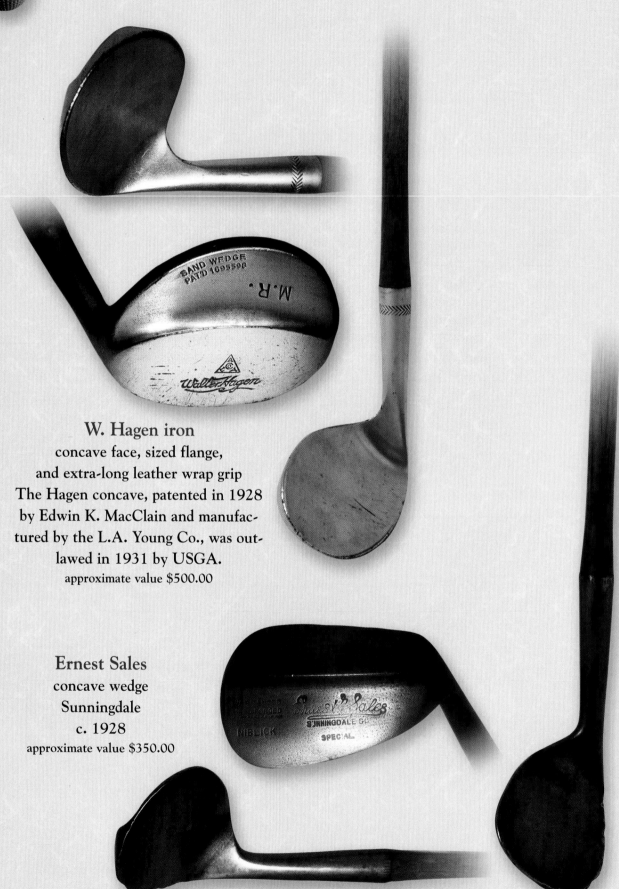

W. Hagen iron
concave face, sized flange,
and extra-long leather wrap grip
The Hagen concave, patented in 1928
by Edwin K. MacClain and manufactured by the L.A. Young Co., was out-
lawed in 1931 by USGA.
approximate value $500.00

Ernest Sales
concave wedge
Sunningdale
c. 1928
approximate value $350.00

Cochrane
"Super Giant" niblick
6½" wide, 4¾" deep
Few exist and it is questionable if any were ever
played. They may have been display samples.
c. 1920s
approximate value $4,500.00

Four Niblicks
From left to right

Winton "Last Word," wood shaft, c. 1907,
approximate value $1,100.00

Spalding, sweet spot No. 19, c. 1930s,
approximate value $110.00

Beckley-Ralston, "398," c. 1930s,
approximate value $110.00

Burr-Key Bilt, copper plug insert at the sweet spot, c. 1930s,
approximate value $105.00

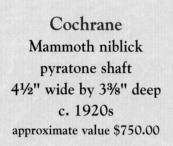

Cochrane
Mammoth niblick
pyratone shaft
4½" wide by 3⅜" deep
c. 1920s
approximate value $750.00

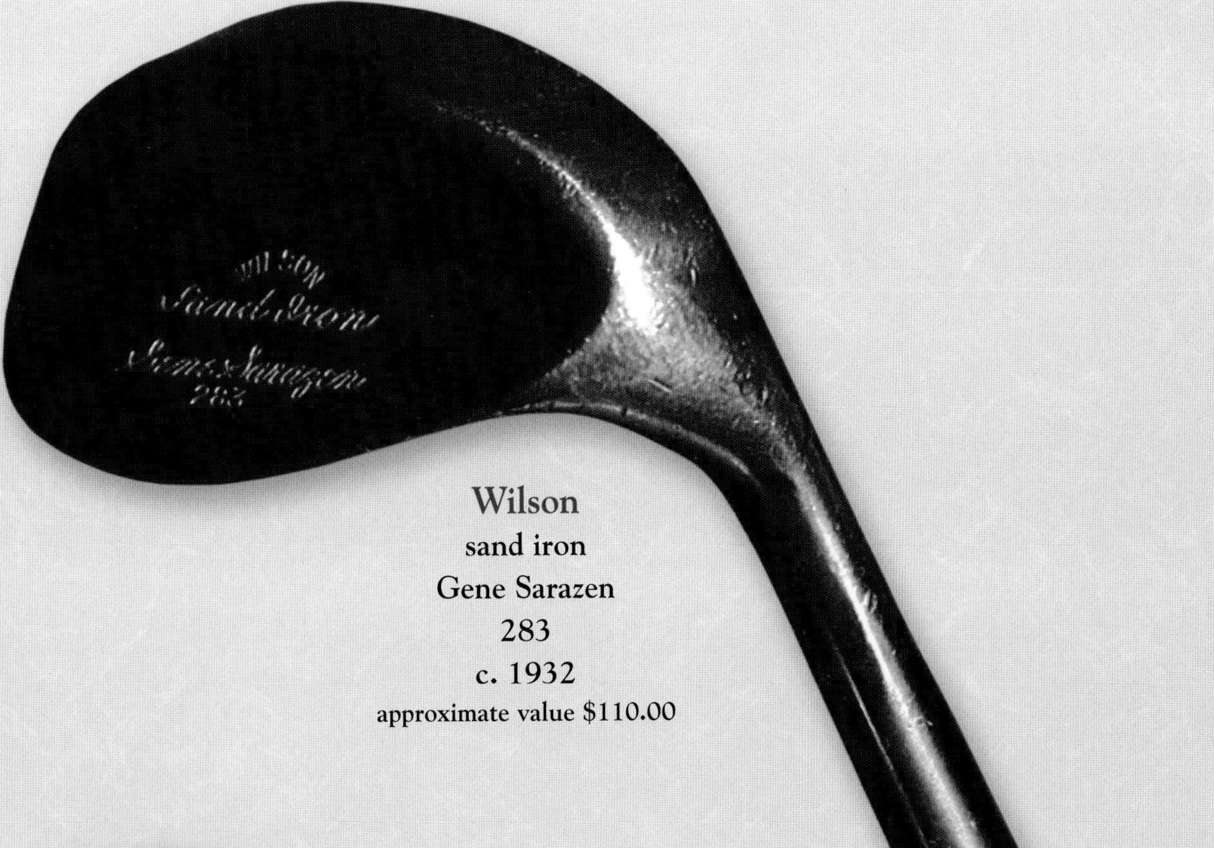

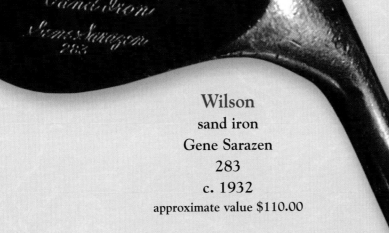

Wilson
sand iron
Gene Sarazen
283
c. 1932
approximate value $110.00

Wilson
R-90
sand iron
pyratone shaft
c. 1933
approximate value $110.00

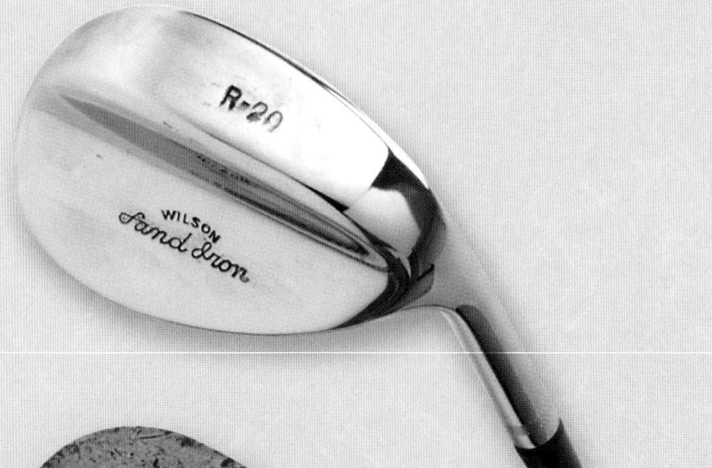

Wilson
"R-20,"
pyratone shaft
c. 1937
approximate value $150.00

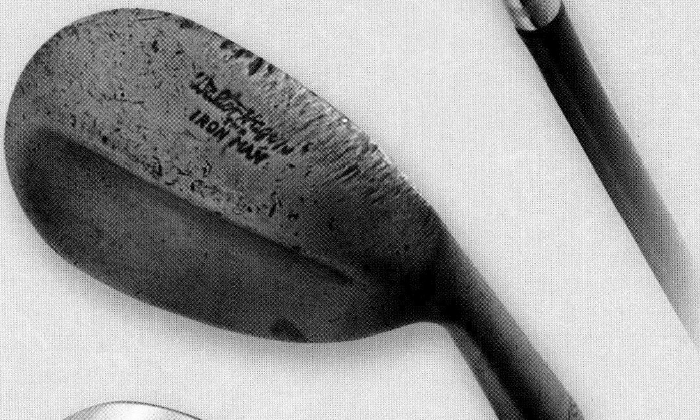

Wilson
Iron Man
pyratone shaft
c. 1933
approximate value $150.00

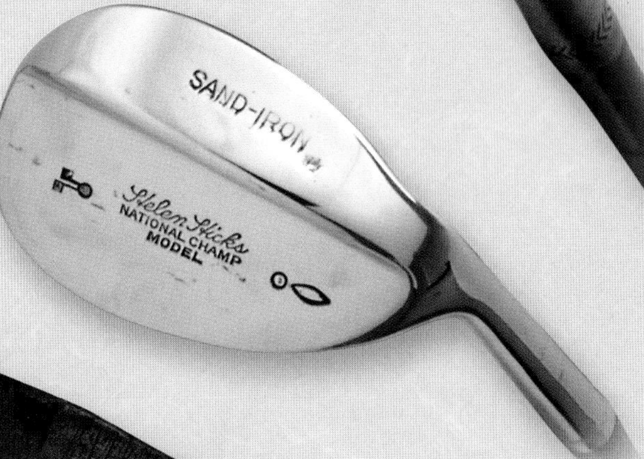

Wilson
Helen Hicks, national champ
pyratone shaft
sand iron, c. 1935
approximate value $150.00

Wilson
"Bomber"
pyratone shaft
c. 1932
approximate value $150.00

Beckley-Ralston
"Skimmer"
pyratone shaft
most concave iron I've seen
c. 1932
approximate value $225.00

MacGregor
"Scooper"
steel shaft
1930s
approximate value $65.00

Vulcan
"Trap Stick"
c. 1930s
approximate value $75.00

George Forrestor
Cleek duplex
hollow V sole
wood shaft
c. 1920s
approximate value $1,100.00

Kroydon
putter – chipper
c. 1930s
approximate value $55.00

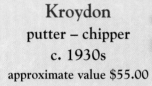

Bristol
"Approacher"
c. 1930s
approximate value $55.00

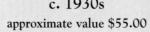

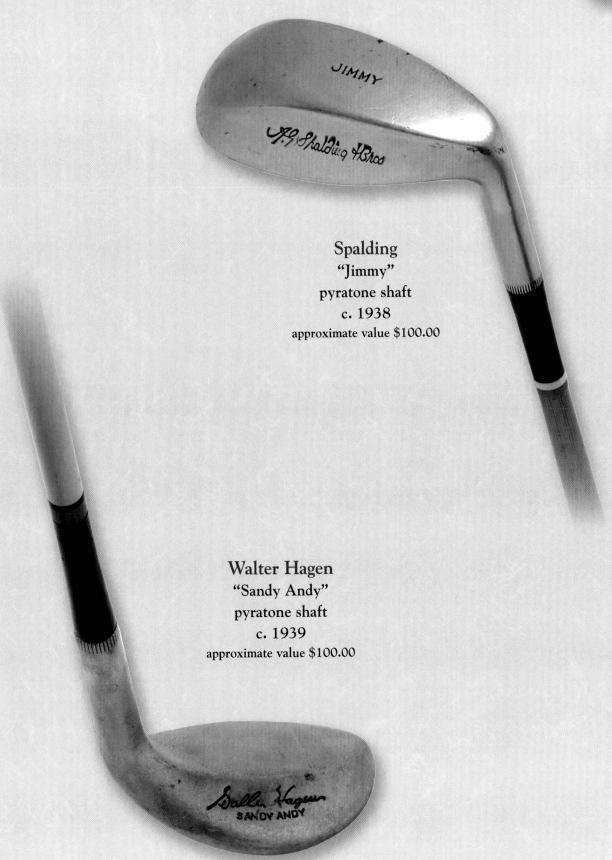

Spalding
"Jimmy"
pyratone shaft
c. 1938
approximate value $100.00

Walter Hagen
"Sandy Andy"
pyratone shaft
c. 1939
approximate value $100.00

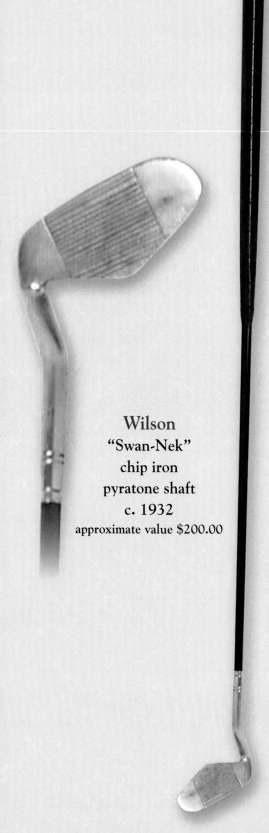

Wilson
"Swan-Nek"
chip iron
pyratone shaft
c. 1932
approximate value $200.00

From top to bottom

Spalding chipper
Spalding chipper
Kroydon
Bristol
Spalding "RU"
Wilson "Chip iron"
Wilson "Chip iron"
"C" represented a ladies' club
c. 1930
approximate value $40.00 each

Burke
Smith iron
c. 1928
approximate value $150.00

A most valuable club where the ball position allowed nothing more than a one hit with a 12-inch long club. Offered by Burke as a "trouble iron" with those developed later bearing the inscription "No Unplayable Ball." This iron went into the 50s and 60s as the "Nub Iron."

MacGregor
"Double Service" wedge
3852 MS
c. 1938
approximate value $75.00

H & B
No. "99" wedge
c. 1940s
approximate value $65.00

Spalding
"The Axe" niblick
anvil C.M., Putney, Eng.
c. 1900s
approximate value $2,100.00

Wedges

From top to bottom

Burke "Save A Shot"
Spalding "Dynamiter"
Wilson "Maycraft"
Spalding "P.D.N."
c. 1920 – 1930s
approximate value $55.00 each

Grooved Irons and Wedges

It remains uncertain whether
Jack White or Ben Sayers
was the inventor of the grooved sole. Each claim
it. Other manufacturers besides them copied it.
c. 1930
approximate value $45.00 each

George Sayers
grooved sole
Niblick
"Bulldozer"
pyratone shaft
c. 1940
approximate value $55.00

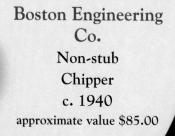

Boston Engineering
Co.
Non-stub
Chipper
c. 1940
approximate value $85.00

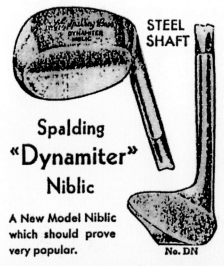

STEEL SHAFT

Spalding "Dynamiter" Niblic

A New Model Niblic which should prove very popular.

No. DN

No. DN. Spalding "Dynamiter" Niblic.

A new model niblic which should prove very popular. This iron is of the orthodox niblic type, but made extra heavy to insure blasting the ball from sand traps and deep grass with a minimum amount of effort. By letting the club head do the work, the player is relieved from the inaccuracy of the strenuous effort which is necessarily put into a blow to get the ball out of a bad lie, thus insuring much better results. Outstanding features of this club are: The short steel shaft, which induces a straight left arm; a sand-blasted Parkerized club face; a Parkerized steel shaft to eliminate any possible sun glare in the eyes when making the shot. This finish also provides a perfect contrast between the ball, the white sand and the club head. The club face of this new iron is slightly concave from heel to toe. From sole to top it is straight, which, as is well known, gives more backspin to the ball than when the face is vertically concave.

Each, **$7.50**

Spalding Catalog

Spalding
"Dynamiter" wedge-niblick
fish scale model
pyratone shaft
c. 1935
approximate value $100.00

Tom Morris Sr.
considered the most revered man in the history of golf. His club
making, playing, and influence on the game was extraordinary.
His clubs from the 1860 long noses to the 1930 pyratone
shafted club pictured above are of the highest quality.
c. 1930s
approximate value $150.00

Practice Clubs

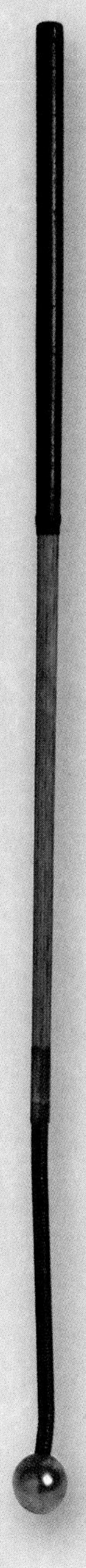

Ernest Jones
"Pro" Swing practice club
product of a great pro,
teacher, writer, and innovator of club designs
c. 1933
approximate value $950.00

Dave Pelz
practice putters
c. 1970s
approximate value $125.00

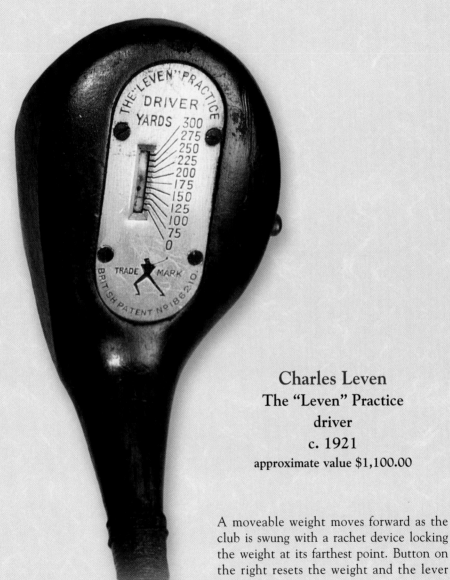

Charles Leven
The "Leven" Practice
driver
c. 1921
approximate value $1,100.00

A moveable weight moves forward as the club is swung with a rachet device locking the weight at its farthest point. Button on the right resets the weight and the lever again starts at zero.

Schenectady
From top to bottom

Pat. Pending 1902, approximate value $700.00
Pat. March 24, 1903, approximate value $400.00
Jerry Travers, 1928, approximate value $225.00

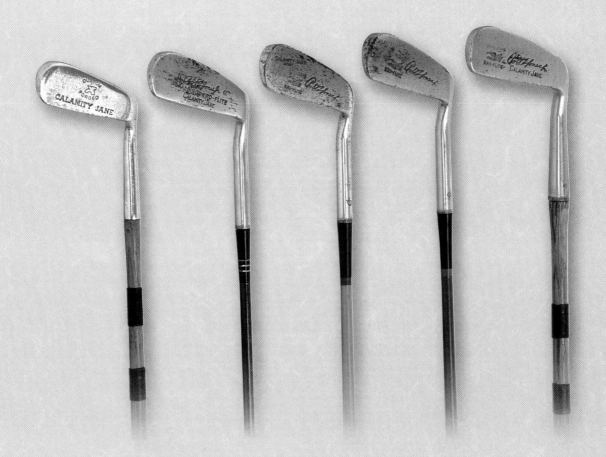

Spalding
Calamity Jane putters
From left to right

wood shaft, custom forged 1960, approximate value $100.00
pyratone shaft, 1937, approximate value $100.00
pyratone shaft, 1935, approximate value $100.00
pyratone shaft, 1939, approximate value $100.00
wood shaft, c. 1934, approximate value $400.00

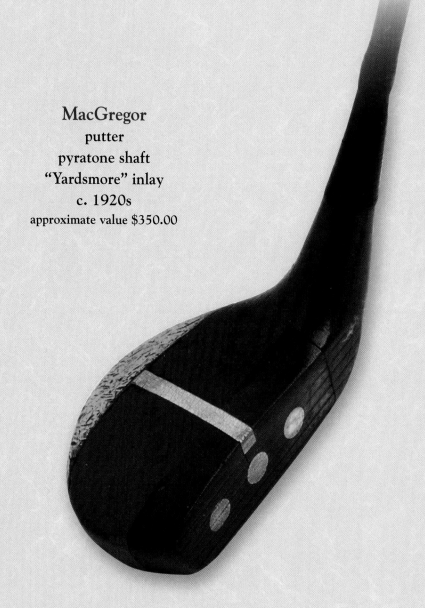

MacGregor
putter
pyratone shaft
"Yardsmore" inlay
c. 1920s
approximate value $350.00

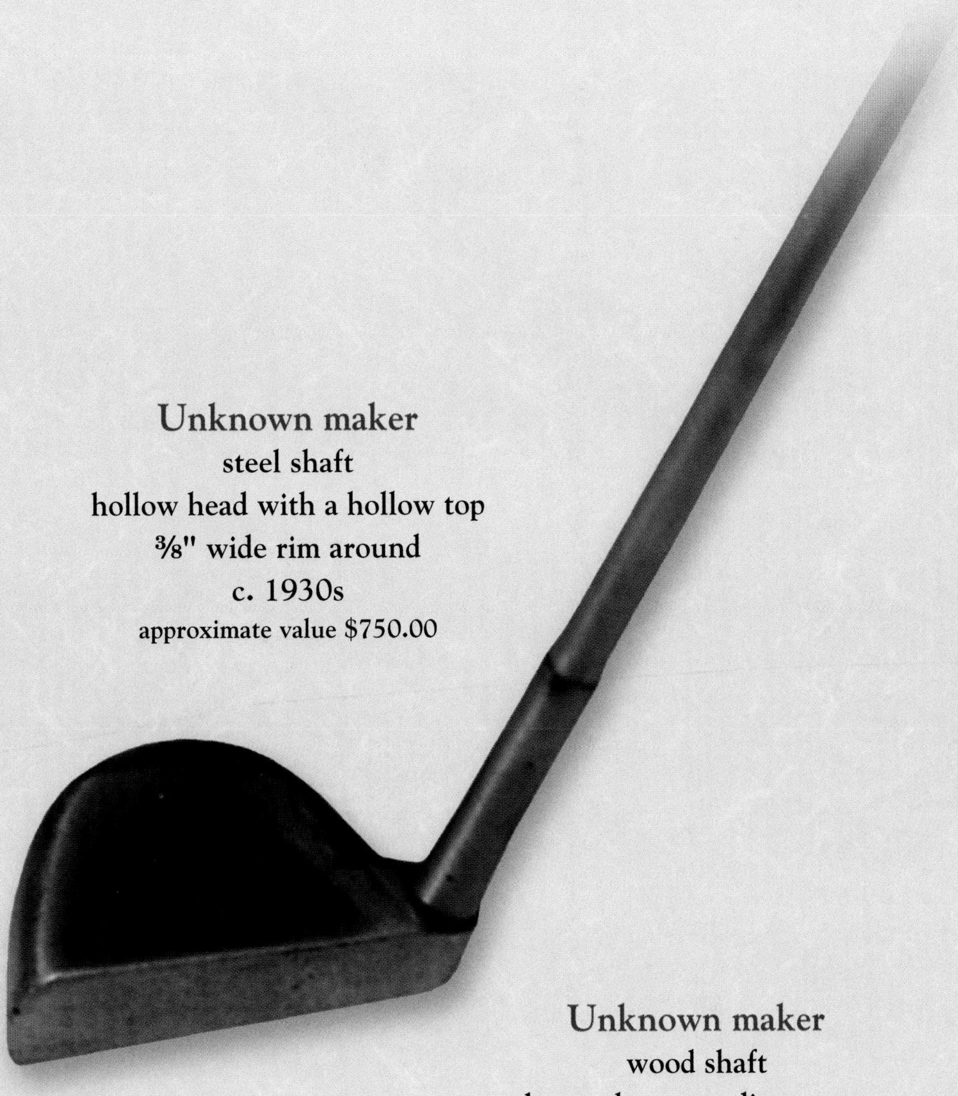

Unknown maker
steel shaft
hollow head with a hollow top
⅜" wide rim around
c. 1930s
approximate value $750.00

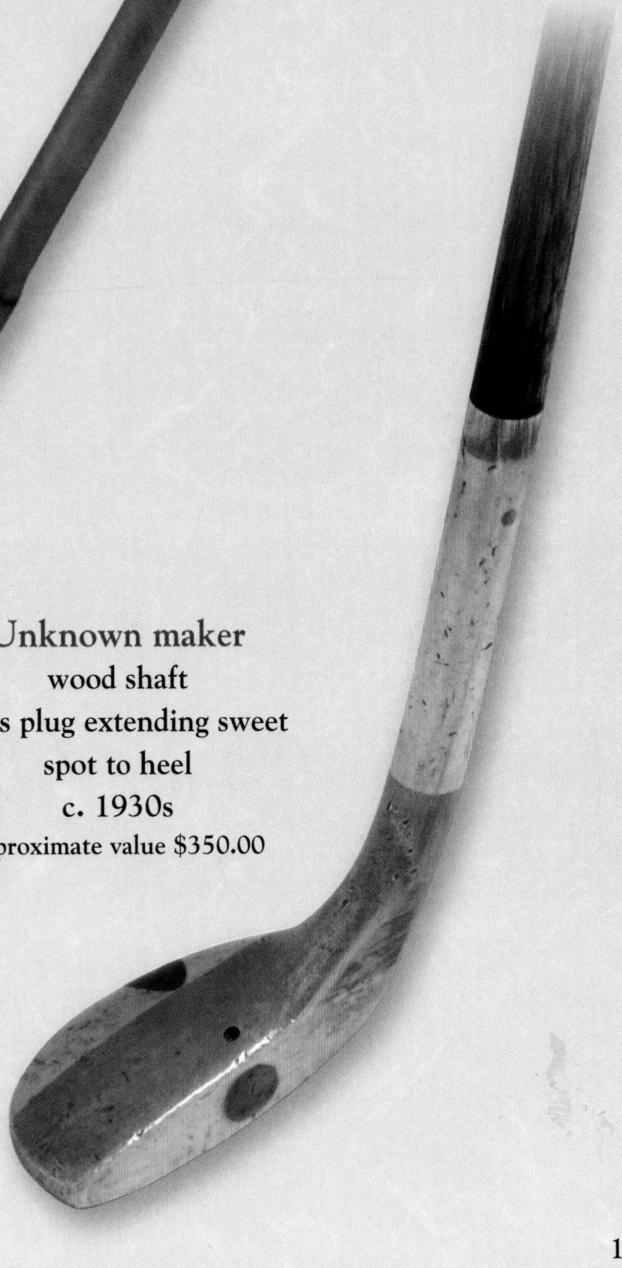

Unknown maker
wood shaft
brass plug extending sweet
spot to heel
c. 1930s
approximate value $350.00

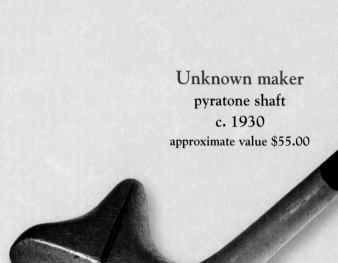

Unknown maker
pyratone shaft
c. 1930
approximate value $55.00

Frank Brady
"Deadly Overspin" putter
convex brass face
hollow back, flat to round hosel
c. 1923
approximate value $800.00

Fred Saunders
"Straight Line"
aluminum putter
wooden shaft
c. 1919
approximate value $950.00

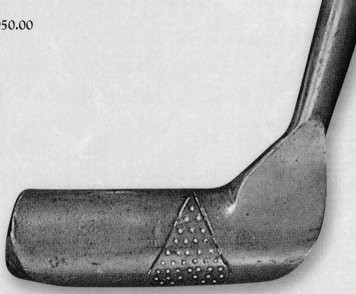

Mac & Mac
pointed back putter
made of German silver with a
square shaft mount to help
the golfer's alignment
c. 1923
approximate value $475.00

Standard Tool
Sta-Put
paddle handle
c. 1940
approximate value $80.00

Unknown maker
"Up Shot" putter
c. 1970s
approximate value $40.00

Hoglund
"Nassal" putter
c. 1950
approximate value $45.00

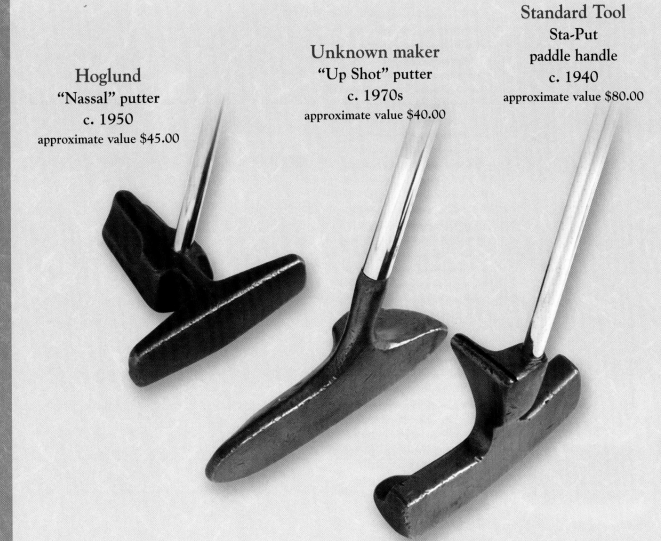

Unknown maker
steel shaft
putter
brass plug insert in face
c. 1930s
approximate value $550.00

A.L. Johnson
wood shaft
bullet shaped pod
putter
c. 1920s
approximate value $1,250.00

Spalding
"Youds" putter
lead insert to place the center of
gravity closer to the ball and also
for a better "feel" when putting
c. 1917
approximate value $450.00

R. Forgan
Maxmo putter
Forganite material
c. 1928
approximate value $185.00

Unknown maker
deep flanged putter with six ¼" rails
a high center of gravity or topspin
roll which would work incredibly
well on greens of the early 1900s
approximate value $1,150.00

Gibson & Co.
King Horn
"Ski Slope" putter
c. 1910
approximate value $850.00

150

Otto Hackbarth
wood shaft
forked hosel
slotted brass or lead insert
c. 1910
approximate value $500.00

J. Ellis in *The Clubmaker's Art* p. 180 quotes *Golfers Magazine*, August 1910: 188, "Otto G. Hackbarth, professional at the Westwood Country Club, St. Louis, has invented a new putter of peculiar design with which he has been doing remarkably accurate work on the greens. It is modeled after the center shafted idea and he claims this prevents the club from turning when the ball is struck, with the result that the ball rolls with an overspin, hugging the ground and going perfectly straight for the hole."

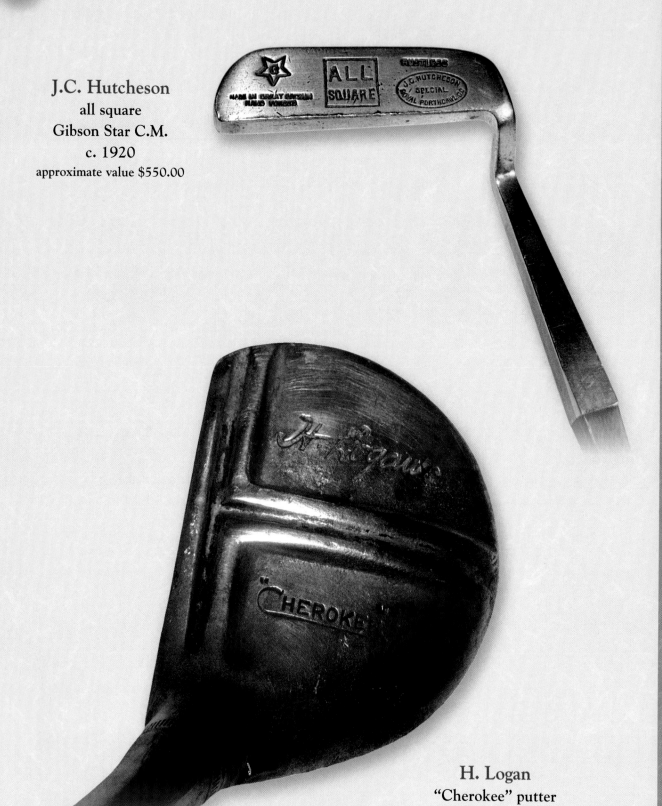

J.C. Hutcheson
all square
Gibson Star C.M.
c. 1920
approximate value $550.00

H. Logan
"Cherokee" putter
wood shaft
c. 1911
approximate value $350.00

Holmac
Rudder putter
with oversized T-shaped brass head
⅜" thick convex brass face
Caruthers hosel
vertical line scoring and leather wrap grip
c. 1922
approximate value $3,500.00

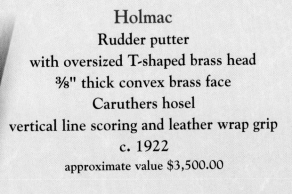

Frank Brady
"Proper stroke" putter
pyratone shaft
c. 1930s
approximate value $150.00

Cosby
"Direct line" putter
steel shaft
c. 1930s
approximate value $300.00

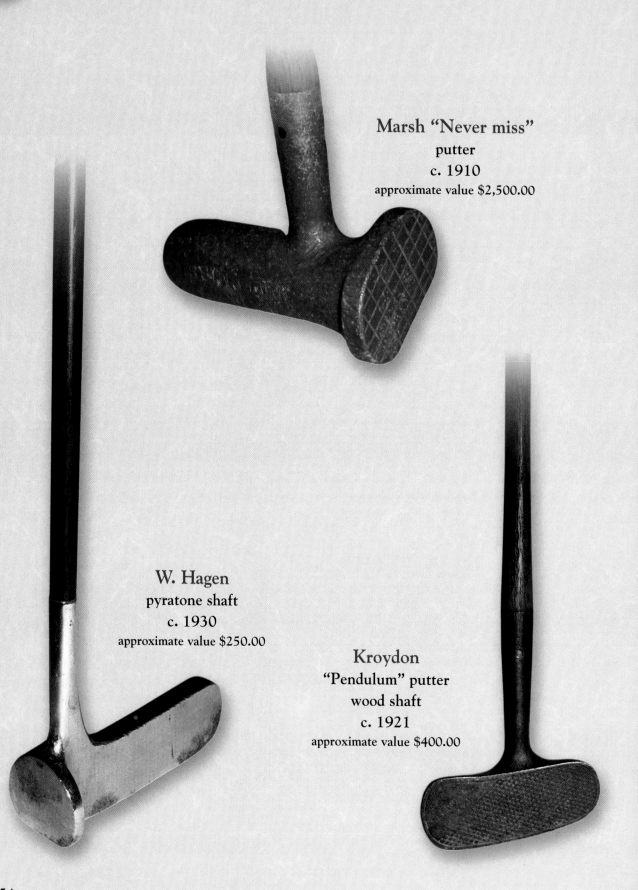

Marsh "Never miss"
putter
c. 1910
approximate value $2,500.00

W. Hagen
pyratone shaft
c. 1930
approximate value $250.00

Kroydon
"Pendulum" putter
wood shaft
c. 1921
approximate value $400.00

J. Randall
mallet putter
pyratone shaft
4½" long head with a ridge running
down the top
12 circular lead plugs spaced in two
rows and inserted in the face
c. 1922
approximate value $210.00

Kroydon
"Aztec" putter
small head
pyratone shaft
semi-mallet
c. 1940
approximate value $50.00

Unknown maker
small head putter
wood shaft
c. 1900s
approximate value $1,500.00

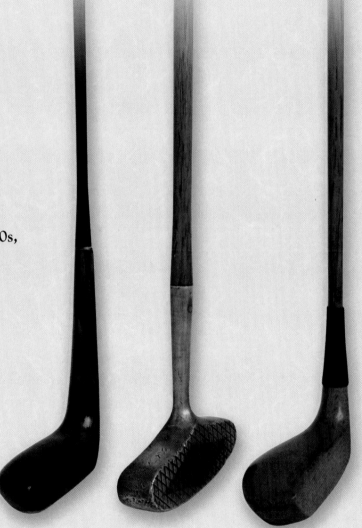

Wilson
putters
From left to right

Small head, 6" hosel, c. 1930s,
approximate value $225.00
Sharpshooter, c. 1920s,
approximate value $375.00
Concave face, c. 1932,
approximate value $255.00

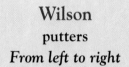

The grip is hollow with four 1½" threaded fingers extending down the shaft. The silver and brass sleeve slid on and tightened them to the shaft at any length up to 7½" beyond its normal 33" length.

Edwin Bacheller
Sure Thing
aluminum with raised triangular sight line
oversized coated steel shaft
According to an advertisement for the club, the shaft is fitted with a telescoping grip that adjusts to give each player the required balance and feel.
putter manufactured in Lynn, Mass., by Sure Thing Products Co.
very heavy club, weighing approximately 19 oz.
c. 1923
approximate value $450.00

Putters
From top to bottom

Volkman mallet
Gene Sarazen long hosel, monel metal
BTN Champion
Pederson "Underslung"
c. 1930s
approximate value $45.00 each

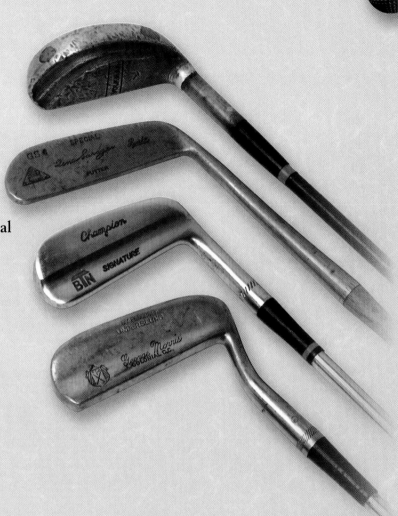

Spalding
"Tru-Focus" putter
⅛" ridge running heel
to toe on back for
sighting aid
c. 1930
approximate value $45.00

D & W Webster
brass insert
sightline stripe
c. 1920s
approximate value $85.00

Ben Sayers
"Rustless"
c. 1940s
approximate value $55.00

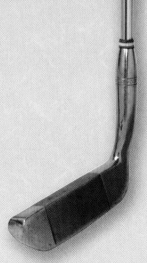

159

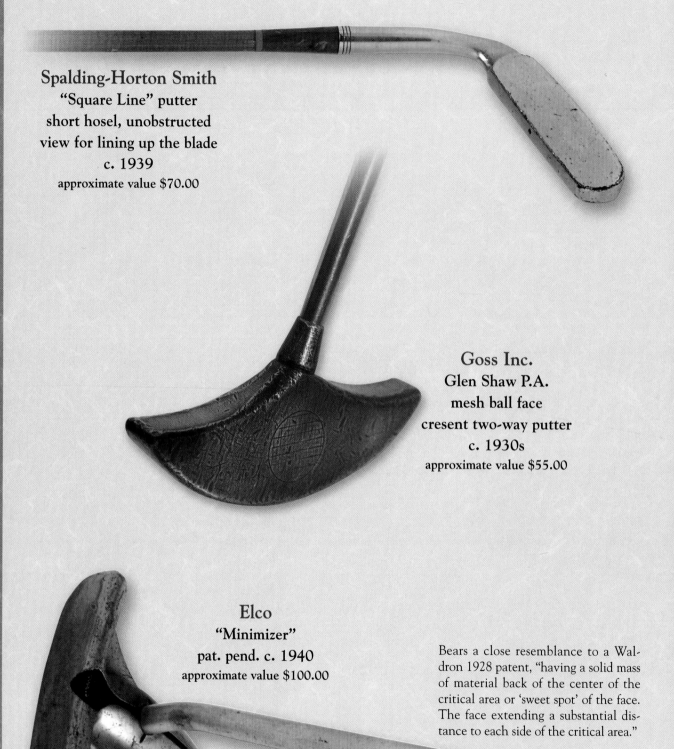

Spalding-Horton Smith
"Square Line" putter
short hosel, unobstructed
view for lining up the blade
c. 1939
approximate value $70.00

Goss Inc.
Glen Shaw P.A.
mesh ball face
cresent two-way putter
c. 1930s
approximate value $55.00

Elco
"Minimizer"
pat. pend. c. 1940
approximate value $100.00

Bears a close resemblance to a Waldron 1928 patent, "having a solid mass of material back of the center of the critical area or 'sweet spot' of the face. The face extending a substantial distance to each side of the critical area."

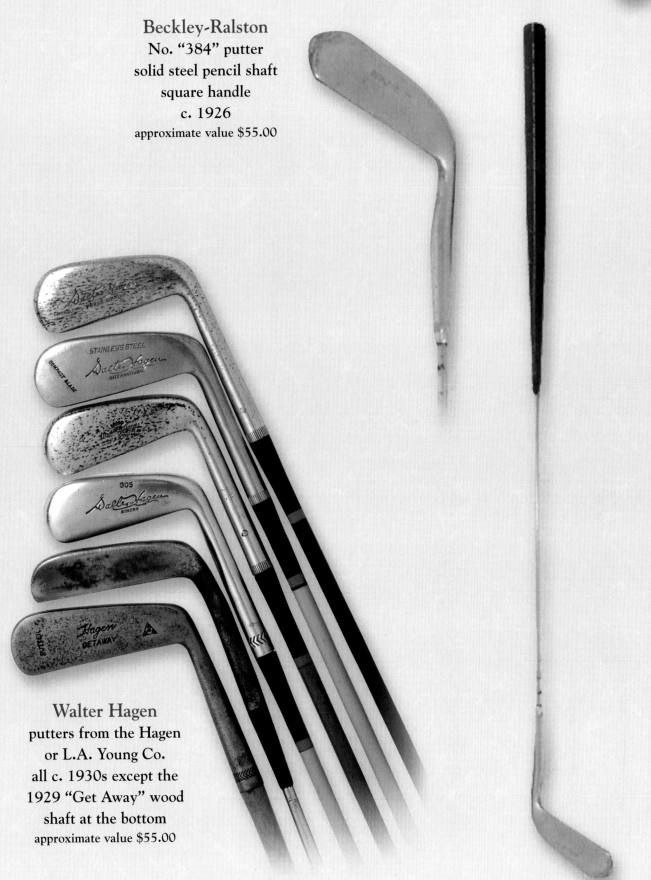

Beckley-Ralston
No. "384" putter
solid steel pencil shaft
square handle
c. 1926
approximate value $55.00

Walter Hagen
putters from the Hagen
or L.A. Young Co.
all c. 1930s except the
1929 "Get Away" wood
shaft at the bottom
approximate value $55.00

Ben Sayers
"In a Class by Themselves"
on shaft label
c. 1940s
approximate value $75.00

Wilson
"Kelly Klub"
c. 1920
approximate value $205.00

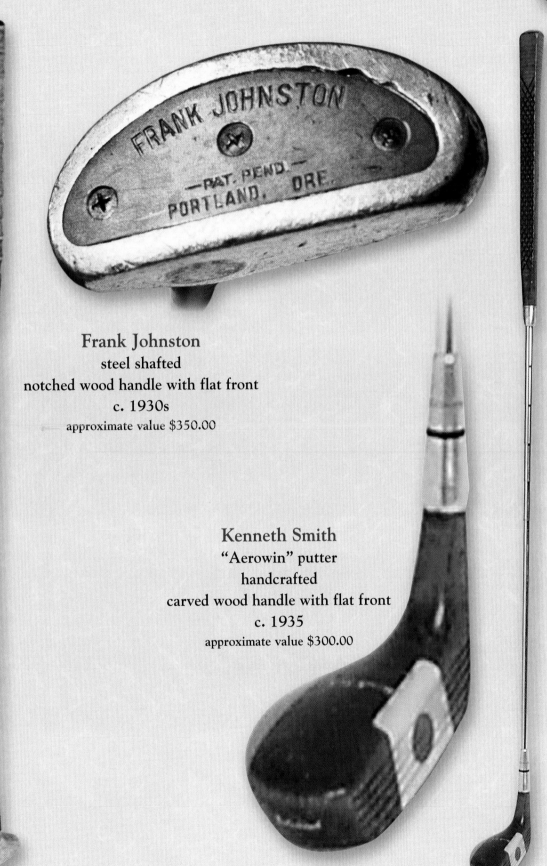

Frank Johnston
steel shafted
notched wood handle with flat front
c. 1930s
approximate value $350.00

Kenneth Smith
"Aerowin" putter
handcrafted
carved wood handle with flat front
c. 1935
approximate value $300.00

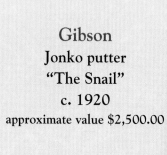

Gassiat
"Grand Piano"
decreases from 1" at the front
edge to ½" at the rear
c. 1913
approximate value $700.00

Gibson
Jonko putter
"The Snail"
c. 1920
approximate value $2,500.00

J.C. Clark
long mallet
c. 1920s
approximate value
$900.00

Frank Johnson Ltd.
"The Frank" putter
c. 1915
approximate value $1,150.00

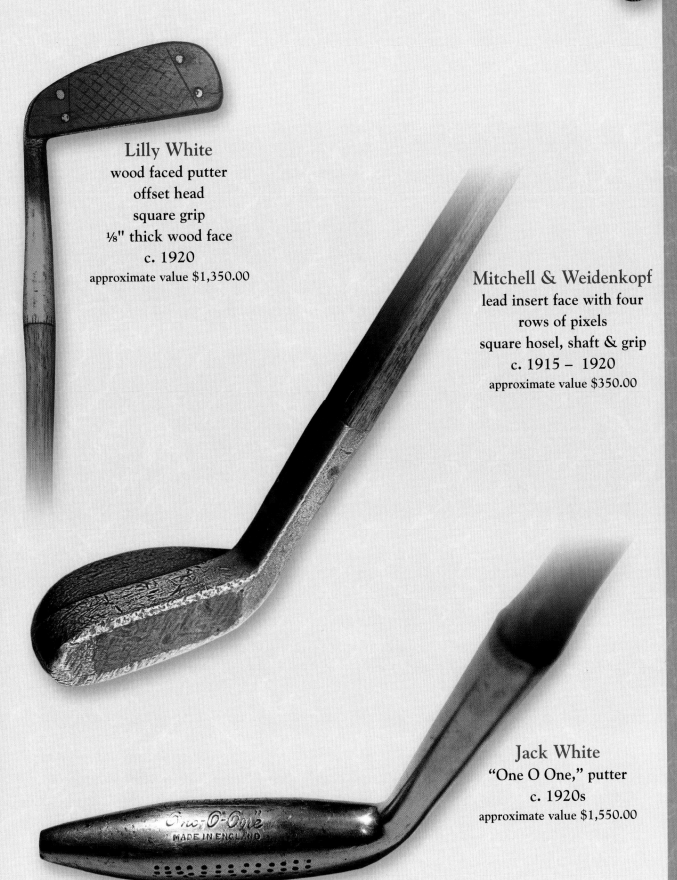

Lilly White
wood faced putter
offset head
square grip
⅛" thick wood face
c. 1920
approximate value $1,350.00

Mitchell & Weidenkopf
lead insert face with four
rows of pixels
square hosel, shaft & grip
c. 1915 – 1920
approximate value $350.00

Jack White
"One O One," putter
c. 1920s
approximate value $1,550.00

Spalding
"Chicopee putter"
wood shaft
c. 1919
approximate value $325.00

Walter Hagen
Lucky Len
wooden mallet head putter
with two rectangular lead
backweights, brass sole, silver
sightlines, and extra long
leather wrap grip
wood shaft
c. 1928
approximate value $275.00

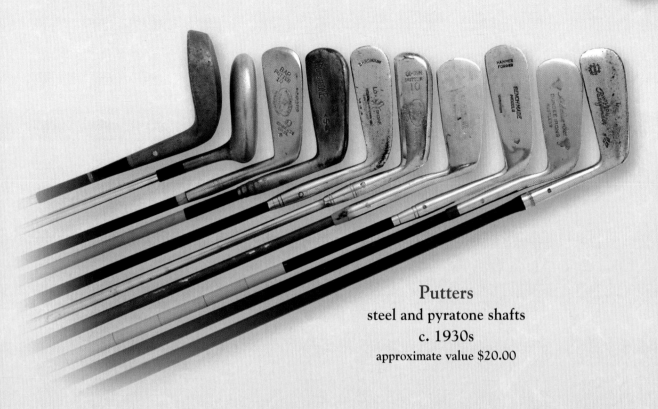

Putters
steel and pyratone shafts
c. 1930s
approximate value $20.00

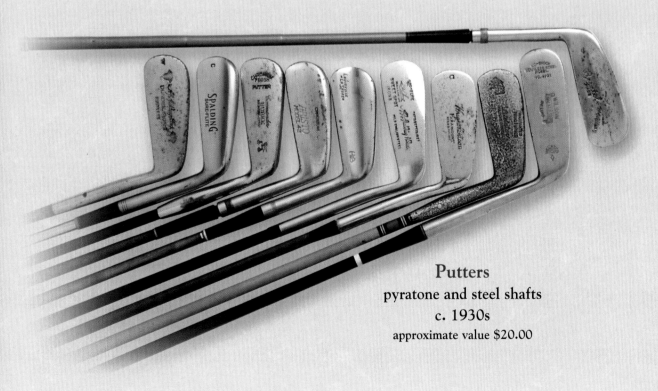

Putters
pyratone and steel shafts
c. 1930s
approximate value $20.00

MacGregor
"Craftsman"
c. 1939
approximate value $175.00

William Harness
solid steel shaft
c. 1928
approximate value
$135.00 each

Bristol
"Juvenile" putters
"The Corporal"
"The Cadet"
pyratone shaft
c. 1933
approximate value
$85.00 each

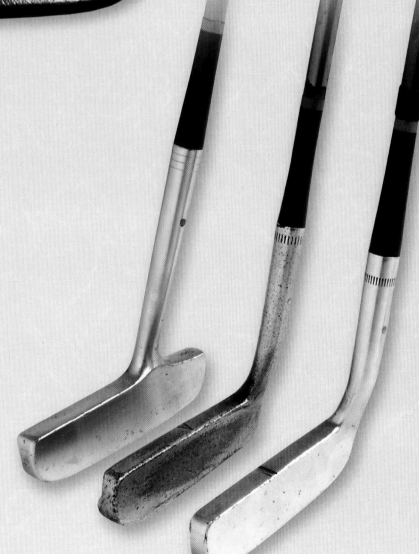

From left to right

MacGregor
Tommy Armour
TDA-40
3852 Series
c. 1930s
approximate value $80.00

Ironmaster
Silverscot
c. 1930
approximate value $80.00

Ironmaster
c. 1930
approximate value $80.00

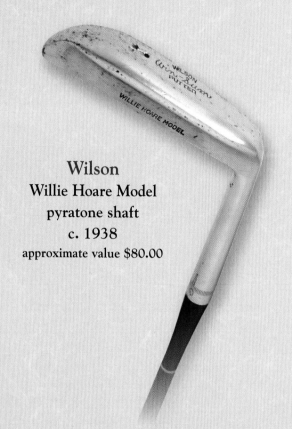

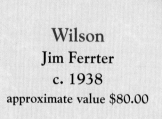

Wilson
Willie Hoare Model
pyratone shaft
c. 1938
approximate value $80.00

Wilson
Jim Ferrter
c. 1938
approximate value $80.00

MacGregor
Jerry Glynn
forerunner of Ironmaster series
c. 1930s
approximate value $80.00

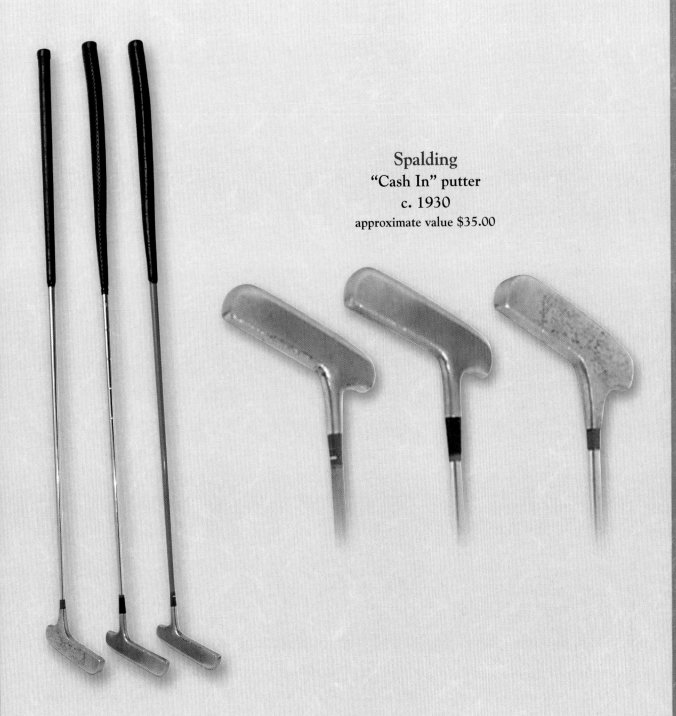

Spalding
"Cash In" putter
c. 1930
approximate value $35.00

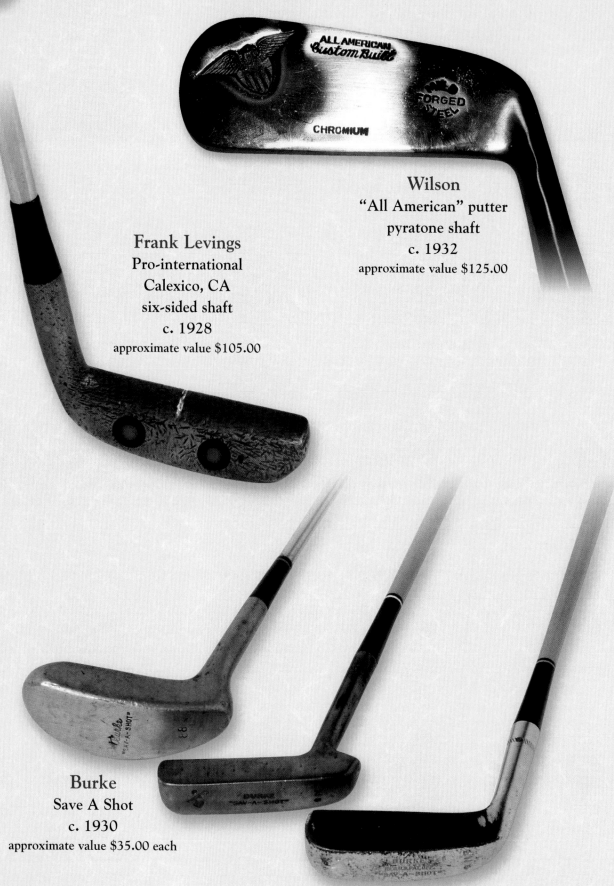

Wilson
"All American" putter
pyratone shaft
c. 1932
approximate value $125.00

Frank Levings
Pro-international
Calexico, CA
six-sided shaft
c. 1928
approximate value $105.00

Burke
Save A Shot
c. 1930
approximate value $35.00 each

From left to right

Ping 1A
approximate value $125.00

Hagen Intruder
approximate value $125.00

Burke Ding-A-Ling
approximate value $125.00

unusual similarity — all
"ringers"
c. 1940 – 1950s

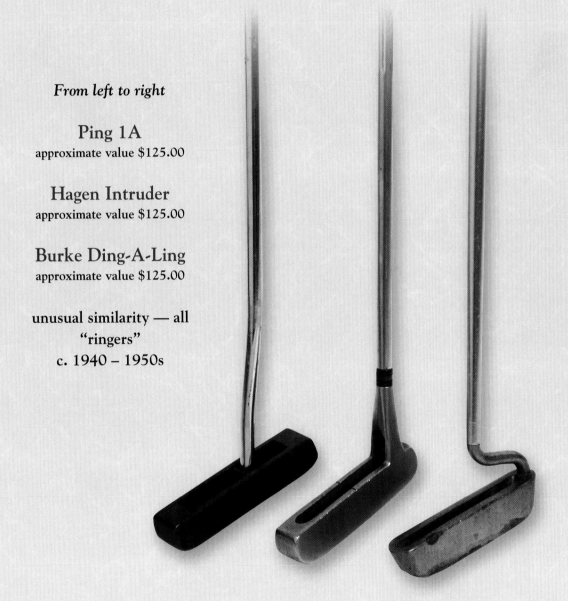

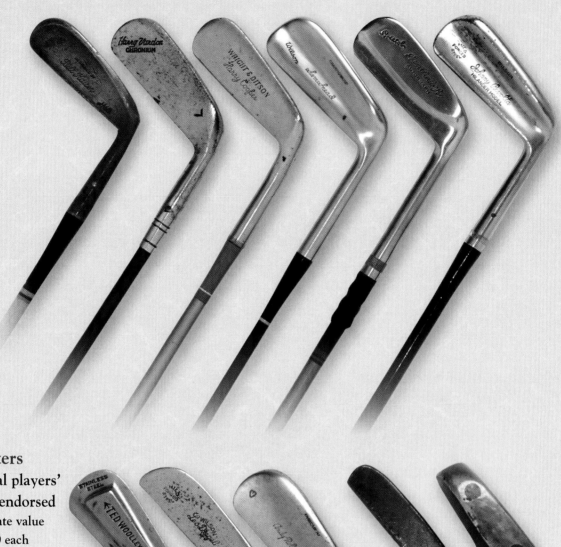

Putters
professional players'
signature endorsed
approximate value
$30.00 each

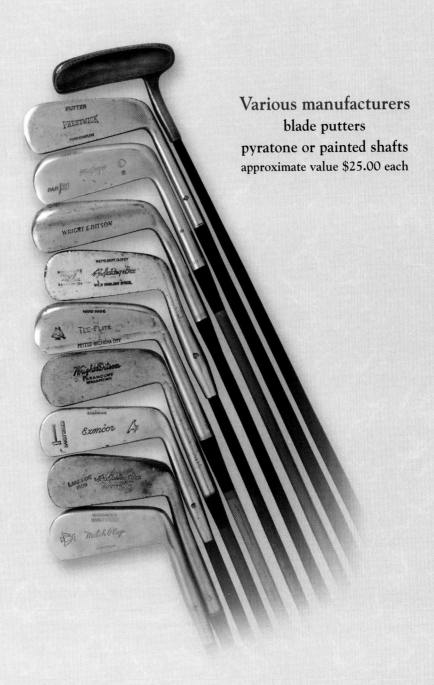

Various manufacturers
blade putters
pyratone or painted shafts
approximate value $25.00 each

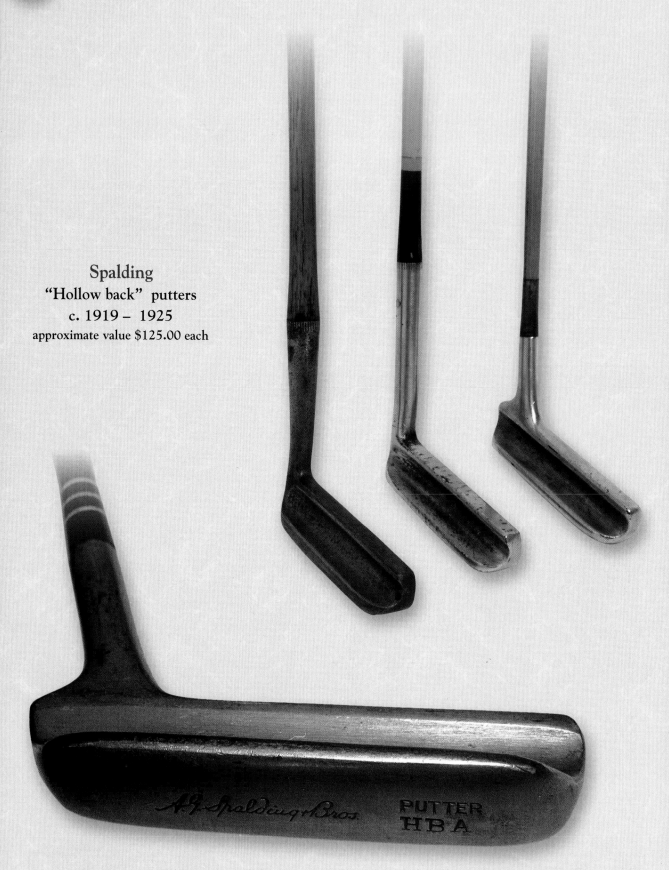

Spalding
"Hollow back" putters
c. 1919 – 1925
approximate value $125.00 each

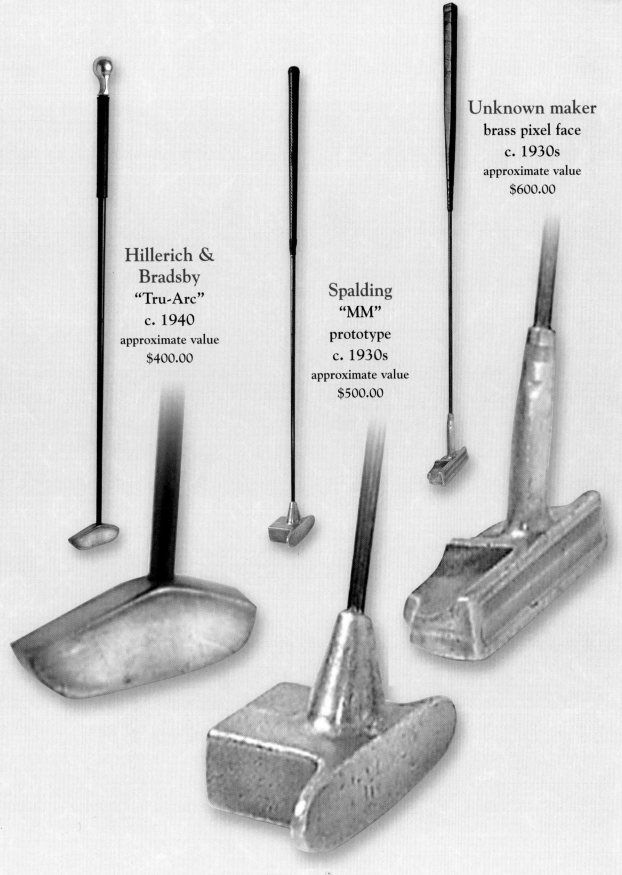

Hillerich &
Bradsby
"Tru-Arc"
c. 1940
approximate value
$400.00

Spalding
"MM"
prototype
c. 1930s
approximate value
$500.00

Unknown maker
brass pixel face
c. 1930s
approximate value
$600.00

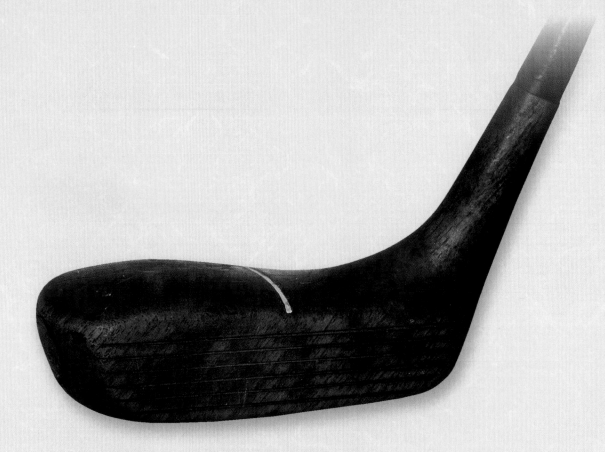

Stan Thompson
Heel & toe weighted putter
hand tailored
c. 1940
approximate value $155.00

Phospher Bronze Smelting Co.
"Kismet" putter
dual side use
c. 1923
approximate value $275.00

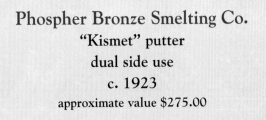

Geo. Cummings
Humpback putter
c. 1920s
approximate value $350.00

Reginald Hincks
offset putter
c. 1929
approximate value $425.00

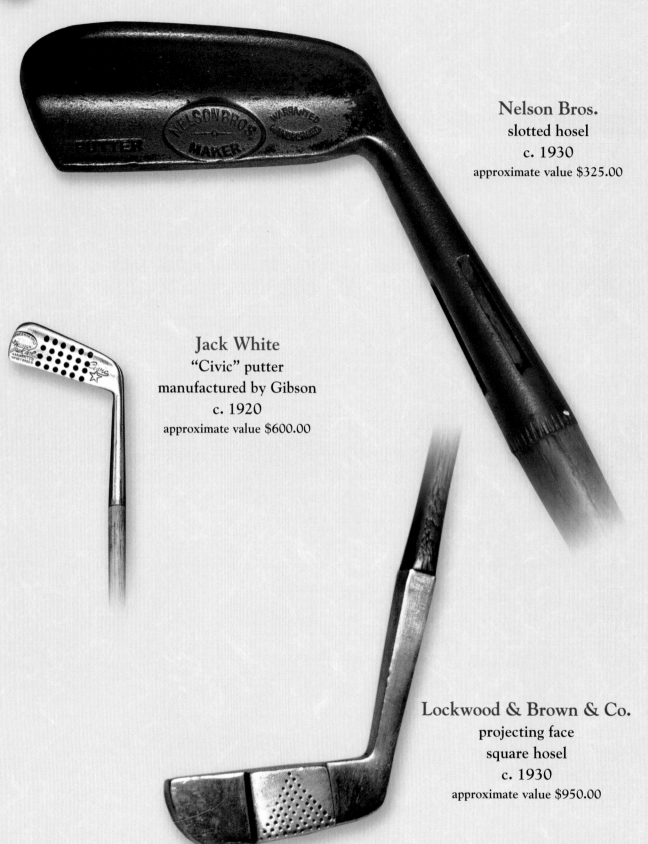

Nelson Bros.
slotted hosel
c. 1930
approximate value $325.00

Jack White
"Civic" putter
manufactured by Gibson
c. 1920
approximate value $600.00

Lockwood & Brown & Co.
projecting face
square hosel
c. 1930
approximate value $950.00

R. Tug Tyler
center shaft
Schnectady style brass face
plate
c. 1920s
approximate value $250.00

MacGregor
"Sink-Em" putter
c. 1922
approximate value $250.00

MacGregor
"Right Angle" putter
c. 1920s
approximate value $250.00

Railed or High Center of Gravity Putters
c. 1920
approximate value
$75.00 each

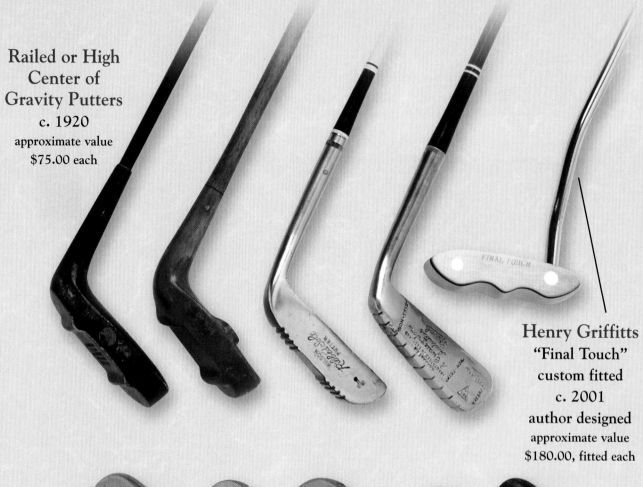

Henry Griffitts
"Final Touch"
custom fitted
c. 2001
author designed
approximate value
$180.00, fitted each

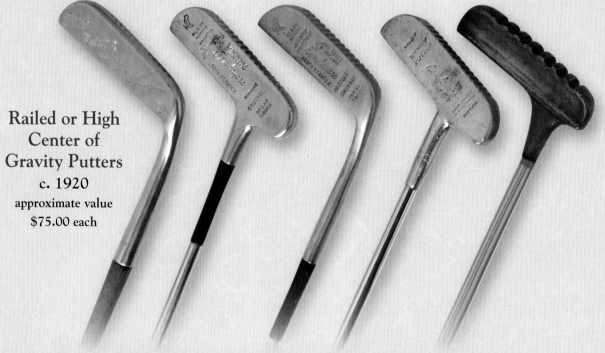

Railed or High Center of Gravity Putters
c. 1920
approximate value
$75.00 each

Albert Percival
Ernest Whitcombe
"Perwhit" putter
c. 1926
approximate value $600.00

The usual premise for a rounded or convex design is that top spin and thus a tighter roll is enhanced.

Wilson
The "Sinker"
c. 1948
approximate value $100.00

MacGregor
"Jack Mallery"
metal shaft
semi-putter
c. 1930
approximate value $125.00

A move toward heel and toe weighting for removing torque when the ball is struck.

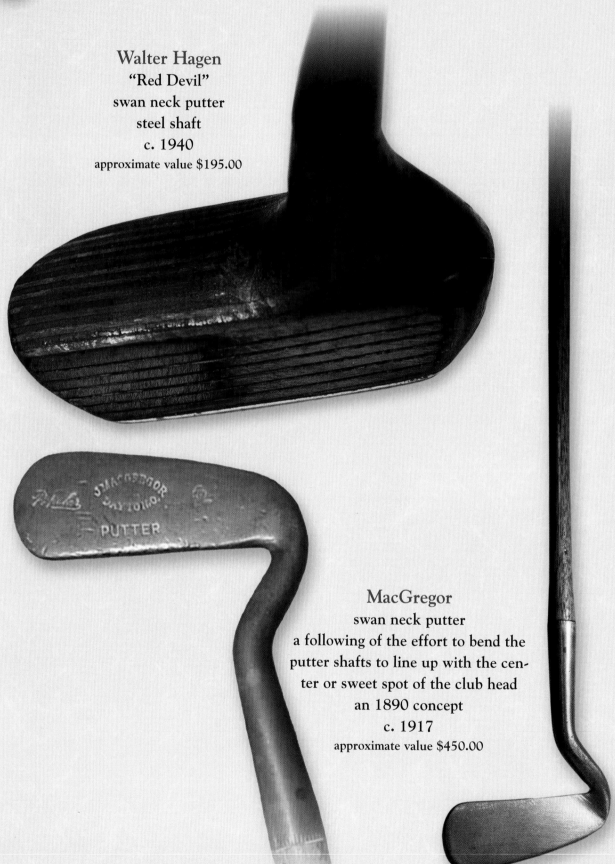

Walter Hagen
"Red Devil"
swan neck putter
steel shaft
c. 1940
approximate value $195.00

MacGregor
swan neck putter
a following of the effort to bend the
putter shafts to line up with the center or sweet spot of the club head
an 1890 concept
c. 1917
approximate value $450.00

Gibson
"Crescent" putter
The extended crescent shape is
just slightly larger than a golf ball.
c. 1920
approximate value $950.00

James Braid
"Orton" putter
Gibson cleek mark
c. 1928
approximate value $175.00

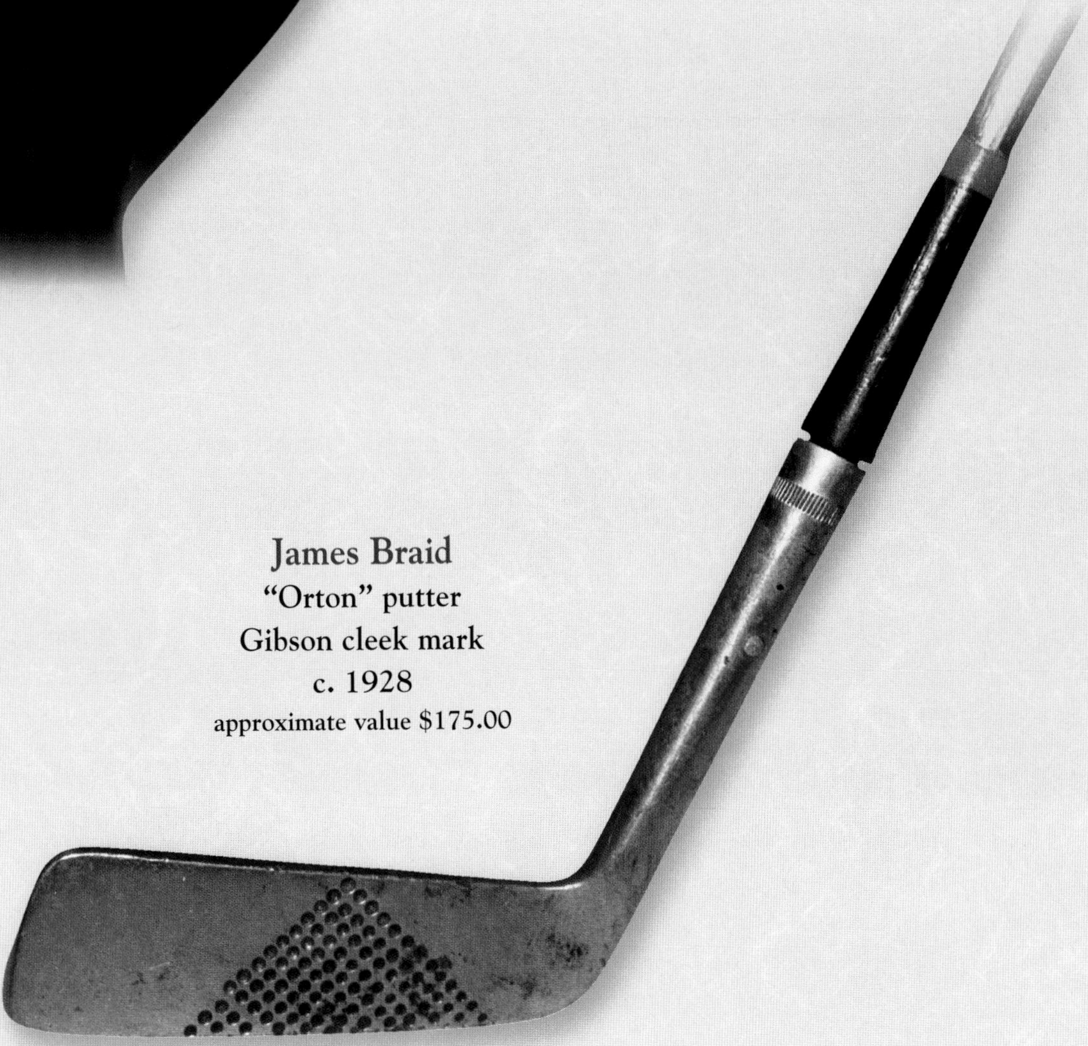

Thistle Putter Co.
"McDougal" T-square putter
"pat pending & Thistle C.M." on sole
face tapers to rear with notched bottom
of T prominent
c. 1914
approximate value $425.00

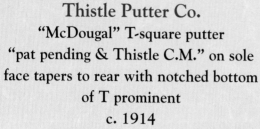

Thistle Putter Co.
"McDougal" T-square putter
patented Jan. 21, 1919, on sole
Thistle cleek mark
approximate value $305.00

Thistle Putter Co.
"McDougal" T-square putter
adjustable weights in two cham-
bers on top of the head with a
spring holding the weights in
place
c. 1919
approximate value $750.00

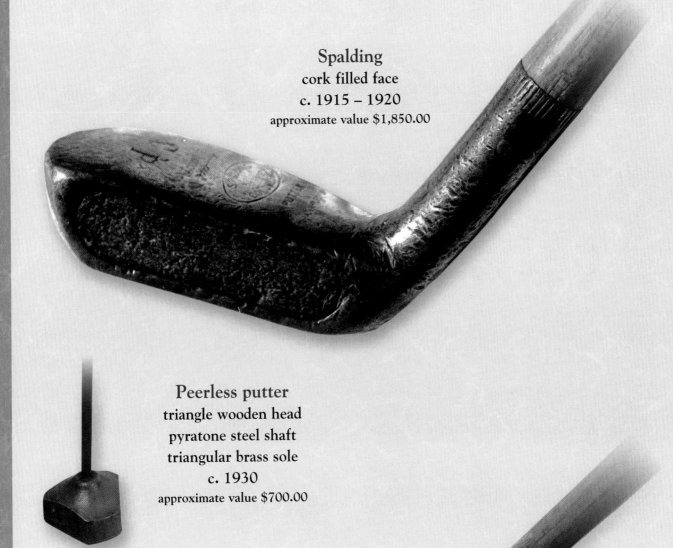

Spalding
cork filled face
c. 1915 – 1920
approximate value $1,850.00

Peerless putter
triangle wooden head
pyratone steel shaft
triangular brass sole
c. 1930
approximate value $700.00

Unknown maker
Diamond head
putter
"C" on top
c. 1920s
approximate value $500.00

Eddy Nunn
Axaline putter
lead weight insert in sole
c. 1950s
approximate value $50.00

Unknown maker
"It's In" putter
c. 1920s
approximate value $120.00

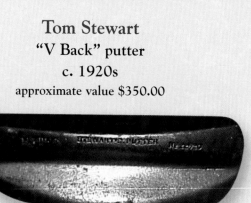

Tom Stewart
"V Back" putter
c. 1920s
approximate value $350.00

Unknown maker
"Level Head"
pat pend on bottom
steel shaft
white paddle grip
c. 1940
approximate value $350.00

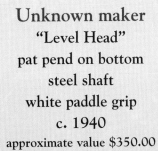

Unknown maker
prototype
features a shaft with a
removable 6", has an aluminum
head with a black synthetic
insert fitting the entire face,
carpenter level in the top
c. 1930
approximate value $600.00

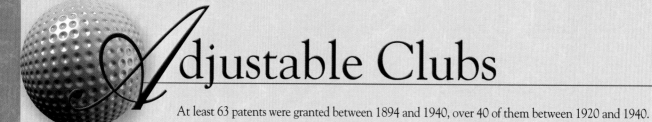

Adjustable Clubs

At least 63 patents were granted between 1894 and 1940, over 40 of them between 1920 and 1940.

James H. Boyes
adjustable putter with aluminum
head, concave back, leather wrap grip
A screw in the head near the hosel
allows the club to be adjusted for loft
for left- or right-handed players.
c. 1922
approximate value $1,000.00

Drakes
"Pendulum" putter
adjust the lie by turning the
head
c. 1949
approximate value $40.00

William W. Davis
"Sprague"
multiface adjustable
putter
c. 1904
approximate value
$1,450.00

Robert Urquhart
adjustable iron
most known of all adjustables
c. 1897
approximate value $2,400.00

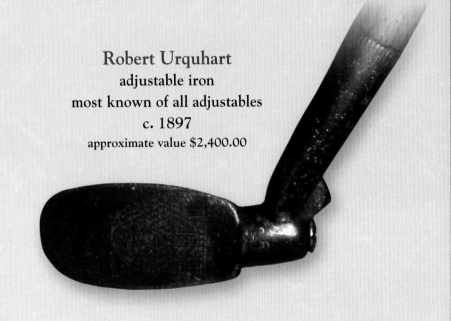

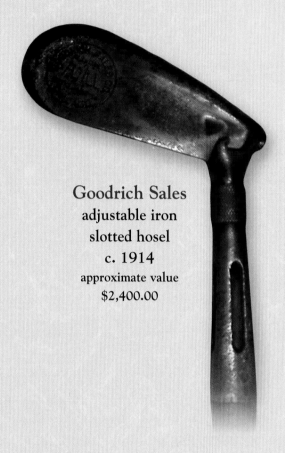

Goodrich Sales
adjustable iron
slotted hosel
c. 1914
approximate value
$2,400.00

Unknown maker
blade can revolve a full 360
degrees allowing any loft
desired
c. 1900s
approximate value $2,500.00

Checkmark
hex screw in the hosel allows
six lofts a putter setting
c. 1957
approximate value $75.00

Miracle
Adjustable
"Traveler"
hexagon shaft
adjusting grip
telescopes to
shorten the club
for traveling
c. 1940
approximate value
$350.00

Detroit Adjustable
pat pending
black steel shaft
early True Temper shaft label
c. 1930
approximate value $250.00

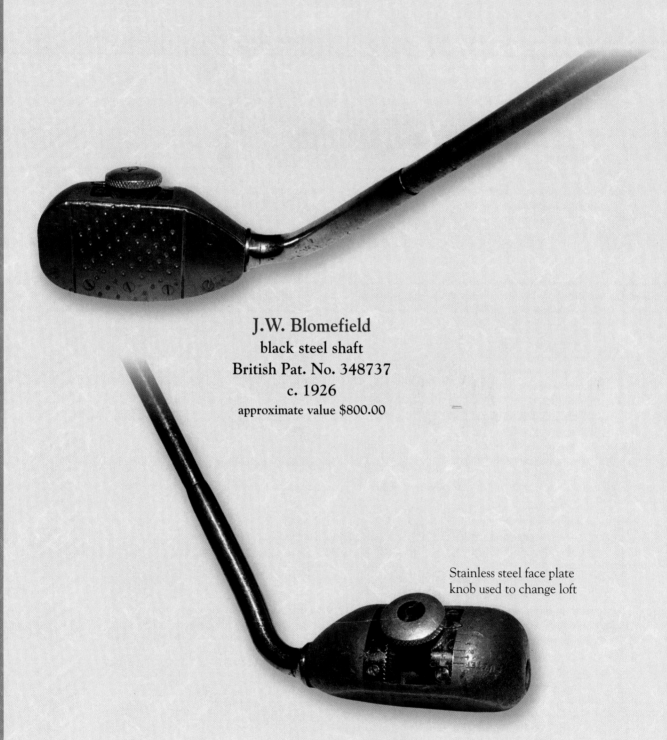

J.W. Blomefield
black steel shaft
British Pat. No. 348737
c. 1926
approximate value $800.00

Stainless steel face plate
knob used to change loft

The Adjustable
steel shaft with brass hosel
c. 1940s
approximate value $115.00

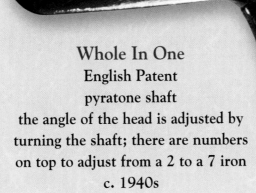

Whole In One
English Patent
pyratone shaft
the angle of the head is adjusted by
turning the shaft; there are numbers
on top to adjust from a 2 to a 7 iron
c. 1940s
approximate value $170.00

From left to right

Glover, c. 1936, approximate value $185.00

Miracle, c. 1944, approximate value $50.00

Miracle, stainless, c. 1944, approximate value $50.00

Mark-Putt, c. 1940s, approximate value $115.00

Novak club, c. 1927, approximate value $185.00

Suit All, Mel Smith, Stan Thompson, c. 1940s, approximate value $45.00

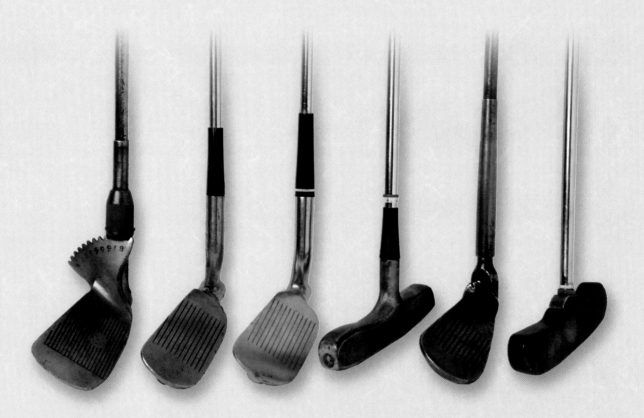

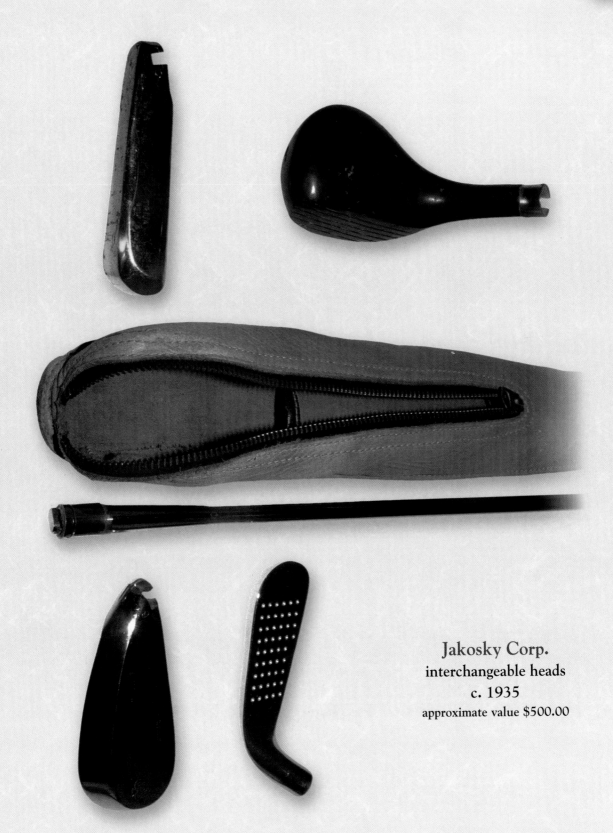

Jakosky Corp.
interchangeable heads
c. 1935
approximate value $500.00

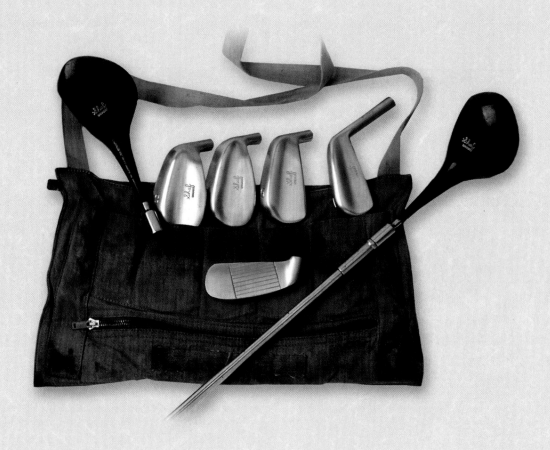

"Shaf"
seven interchangeable heads
c. 1930s
approximate value $600.00

"Portoclub"
eight interchangeable
heads
c. 1950
approximate value $400.00

Grips

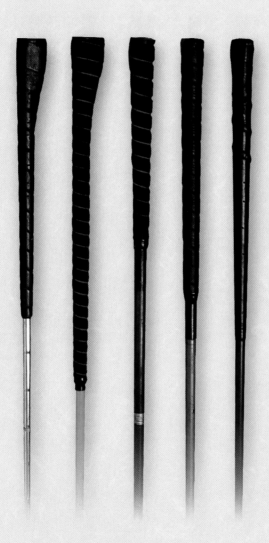

From left to right

- Leather paddle handle grip
- Rubber overwrapping paddle grip
- Rubber, red and black overlapping grip
- Leather overlap grip; flat side not shown; lower round side is in the picture
- Wilson Ridge Runner, c. 1941

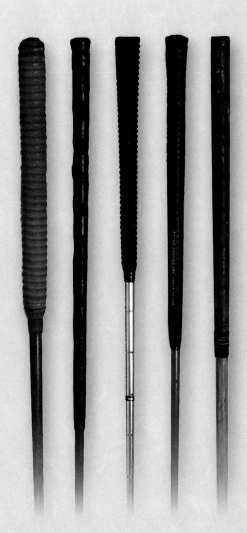

From left to right

- Streamline Putter, hard circular ridged grip
- Alternating cork and leather
- Golfpride grip, composite
- Leather paddle handle
- H & B "Kork" grip, c. 1927

From left to right

- Reminder grip
- Square leather wrap
- English python grip
- Whitcombe Avon India Rubber Co.

From left to right

- (Poss) form fitted grip
- Spalding form fitted grip
- Sewed leather seam on a Bussey club
- Oversized leather paddle handle

From top to bottom

- Goodwin Flange wrap
- Cooper grooved grip
- Leather ½ round, front is flat
- Horton grip

From top to bottom

- Leather square grip
- English grip
- Wooden carved, flat side to front grip
- Alternating cork and leather grip

Shafts

Archie Compston
"Bent shaft"
known as the
"St. Andrew's Bend"
and commonly bent by
users of straight wooden
shaft putters
This putter, with its flat
grip, was patented in 1926.
approximate value $1,250.00

MacGregor
forked shaft putter
lower edge has a ³⁄₁₆
metal insert surrounding
the entire face
developed to reduce
twisting of the head in
striking the ball
c. 1900
approximate value $2,500.00

Wright & Ditson
Harry Cooper
c. 1930

Wright & Ditson
Lawson Little decal
c. 1930s

From left to right

- W. Hagen, spiral shaft, c. 1930s
- Bristol, "Pyramid," six-sided pyratone shaft, c. 1933
- Northwestern, slat shaft, c. 1938

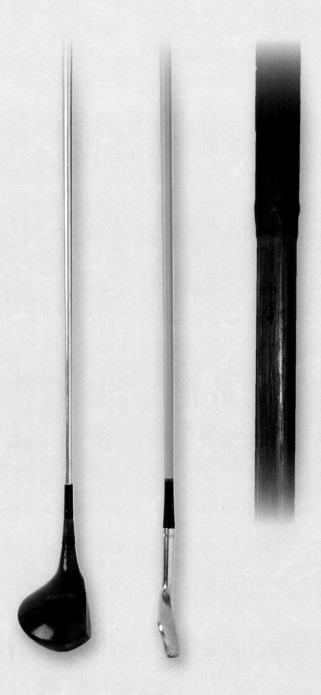

From left to right

• MacDonald Bilt, teardrop shaft, patented in 1929 and used by many manufacturers, has a ridge running down the opposite side of the impact line or face, c. 1940
• Wilson, hex or six-sided shaft, c. 1940
• H & B, Stewart Maiden B Bow shaft, c. 1928

GoldSmith
"Precision-Built" Golf Clubs

The Goldsmith Golf Line for 1938 embodies new and advanced ideas which have been tested and proven by many leading professionals and have been found to be sound and practical in actual play. Only the finest materials are used in their construction. Weight, lie, loft, and balance are scientifically determined. Painstaking and exacting workmanship is paramount in producing the finest clubs that money can buy.

"Swinging Weight" Control

"Swinging Weight" Control is the scientific distribution of the weight of the club. "Swinging Weight" Control, determined with the Lorythmic Golf Club Matching Scale, is based on sound engineering principles and has been thoroughly proven in actual play. **All Goldsmith registered wood and iron sets are definitely checked for "Swinging Weight".**

"Air-Cooled" Grips

A patented grip which permits free circulation through the shaft at the gripping point. The leather grip and the top of the cap are drilled to permit free and constant circulation of air (see diagram). "Air-Cooled" grips afford a firmer hold by preventing slippage caused by excessive moisture and perspiration. They give a feeling of added security in making shots.

"Air-Cooled" Grip

GOLF CLUB SHAFTS

Many golfers have individual ideas as to golf shafts, and in order to provide a selection for those who have special preferences, we have incorporated five different types in the 1938 line: Goldsmith "Spring-Action", "True Temper", Straight Tapered, the new Fox and English "Graded Whip" Shafts.

"SPRING-ACTION" SHAFTS. A patented exclusive Goldsmith shaft with a "Spring-Action" spiral coil placed at the correct and scientifically determined flexing point. Gives the correct amount of flexibility; vibrationless and shockless feel; dissipates shaft strain; adds additional distance.

"TRUE TEMPER" SHAFTS. A shaft made in a series of step-downs which govern the amount of flexibility or stiffness. The shaft is tapered throughout its length to cut down air resistance and step up the speed of the club head.

STRAIGHT TAPERED SHAFTS. A sturdy shaft with tapered thickness of the side walls regulated to obtain the desired amount of feel and flexibility.

FOX DOUBLE TAPERED SHAFTS. An English type shaft very much in demand. Built with a double taper, it flexes directly beneath the grip and above the club head. Fox Shafts give you a definite "feel" of the club head, greater control, as well as added power and distance.

"GRADED WHIP" SHAFTS. Designed by Archie Compston, famous English Professional. The Whip in the shaft is placed at a scientifically pre-determined point which gives greater flexibility, better control, without excessive torque.

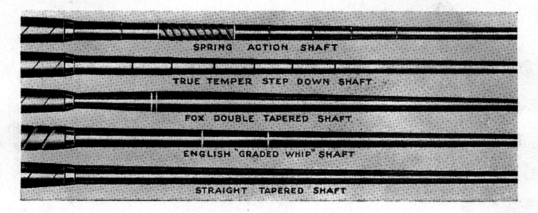

SPRING ACTION SHAFT

TRUE TEMPER STEP DOWN SHAFT

FOX DOUBLE TAPERED SHAFT

ENGLISH "GRADED WHIP" SHAFT

STRAIGHT TAPERED SHAFT

1938 Goldsmith Catalog

Collector's Choice (Tommy Armour)

Tommy Armour was a great golfer and teacher. Clubs bearing his name lead all others bearing golfers' signatures as collectible clubs. Generally they are MacGregor clubs but wood shafted Great Lakes Co., Forgan, Davaga, Shaler, Tom Stewart, and pyratone shafted Burke and Spalding also bear his signature. The Iron Master putters and Tourney series clubs by MacGregor bearing his name have been the most collectible.

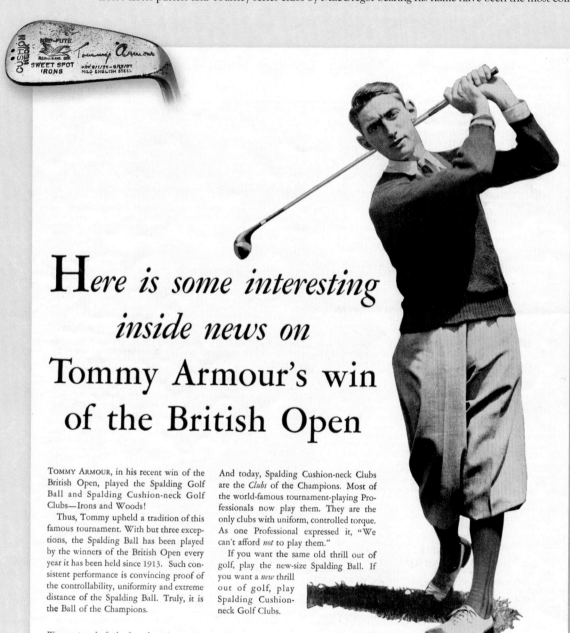

Here *is* *some interesting* *inside news on* Tommy Armour's win of the British Open

TOMMY ARMOUR, in his recent win of the British Open, played the Spalding Golf Ball and Spalding Cushion-neck Golf Clubs—Irons and Woods!

Thus, Tommy upheld a tradition of this famous tournament. With but three exceptions, the Spalding Ball has been played by the winners of the British Open every year it has been held since 1913. Such consistent performance is convincing proof of the controllability, uniformity and extreme distance of the Spalding Ball. Truly, it is the Ball of the Champions.

And today, Spalding Cushion-neck Clubs are the *Clubs* of the Champions. Most of the world-famous tournament-playing Professionals now play them. They are the only clubs with uniform, controlled torque. As one Professional expressed it, "We can't afford *not* to play them."

If you want the same old thrill out of golf, play the new-size Spalding Ball. If you want a *new* thrill out of golf, play Spalding Cushion-neck Golf Clubs.

We are proud of the fact that Armour is a member of the Spalding Field Advisory Staff—a group of leading golfers retained to carry out Spalding's policy of testing in actual play, as well as in the laboratory.

A. G. Spalding & Bros.

· 115 ·

© 1931, A. G. S. & BROS.

Advertisement (1931 *Fortune Magazine*)

211

Great Lakes putter
c. 1929
approximate value $100.00

Tommy Armour prototype
splice neck, possibly by Shaler,
c. 1920s
approximate value $3,500.00

Burke Fancy Face driver
c. 1940s
approximate value $125.00

Tom Stewart 4 Iron
c. 1920s
approximate value $125.00

Tom Thumb Golf Courses

Tom Thumb

The original Tom Thumb Golf Course, located in Chattanooga, Tennessee, was the first patented miniature golf course. It was the creation of Garnet and Frieda Carter. They officially formed the partnership of eccentric whimsey with golf gamesmanship that miniature golf courses have followed ever since. (The Carters also created Rock City, perhaps the most popular roadside attraction in history.) Thousands — the young and old, rich and poor — played the little "courses" (seen on the following page) during the Depression as the prices of regular courses were prohibitive. Although the golf world separates itself from putt-putt and whimsical golf courses, we must all be grateful for this creation. It kept golf accessible and affordable and its extreme popularity focused more of the spotlight on golf.

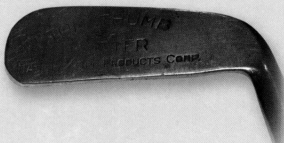

164   THE SATURDAY EVENING POST   May 3, 1930

TOM THUMB GOLF

U. S. Patent Nos.
253,949; 1,559,520
Other Patents Pending

A NEW
outdoor game

BIG PROFITS
for you – –

MILLIONS WILL PLAY

Here is just the outdoor golf game all America has been waiting for. With millions of American golf fans waiting to play—with millions more anxious to learn, the Tom Thumb Miniature Golf Course offers you a most profitable opportunity.

Here's the big idea. The Tom Thumb Golf Game is a complete 18 hole course with tees, greens, hazards, all complete. No two holes are alike. All you need is a well located lot of any shape—60 feet by 120 feet will do—the larger the better—install your Tom Thumb Course and instantly the crowds flock in and start to pay you a profit.

You'll be amazed at the immediate play you will enjoy. For America is golf crazy and a large part of America is already sold on Tom Thumb Golf. They play in bathing suits—in evening clothes—in shirt sleeves—the old—the young—the rich—the poor. Everyone is doing it and making big money for scores of Tom Thumb owners.

Here is instant golf. The public need no preparation. They need no special clothes—no special shoes—no clubs—no balls. They merely walk up to your gate—buy a ticket—you give them a putter and a ball and the fun begins for them and the profit begins for you.

The play is constant—night and day.

The Charleston Miniature Golf Company of Charleston, S. C., write as follows:

"Beg to advise that we have had excellent success with the Tom Thumb Golf Course. We operated this course for one month and our proceeds that month were $2800."

The Greensboro Golf Course, Inc., of Greensboro, N. C., write as follows:

"In reply to your recent inquiry, I beg to state that the receipts of the TOM THUMB GOLF COURSE in Greensboro have been in excess of $1500.00 for the fifteen days that we have been operating."

Hundreds of Tom Thumb Courses are making big money.

Heretofore outdoor miniature golf courses were impractical on account of the wear on the grass. For regular grass, no matter how fine the quality, will not stand the daily grind of hundreds of golfers. But with Tom Thumb Golf a new type of green is furnished. It is called the Tom Thumb Green, the base of which is cotton seed hulls. This is specially mixed and prepared so that it feels like grass, looks like grass—the putting action is the same as on grass and it improves with age. Tom Thumb Greens are patented. This is an exclusive feature.

So when you want to play miniature golf in your town and enjoy it to the full, play on the Tom Thumb Course—the only miniature golf course that can use this patented type of putting green.

Here is your opportunity. With a small amount of capital you can set yourself up in the golf business for the coming season and reap the big profits. Go in for yourself—or take a pal in as a partner—or just the thing for man and wife. Keeps you out of doors and makes you an exceptional return on your investment in the bargain.

Profitable in towns of 5,000 population and up.

From three to six days after you receive the Tom Thumb Course you can be operating. Easy to install. Write at once for full details. Don't overlook this unusual opportunity. Address the nearest office listed below. And wire or write right now!

Fairyland Manufacturing Co.
Chattanooga, Tenn.

National Pipe Products Corp.
Rochester, Penna.

Tom Thumb Sales Corp.   Tom Thumb Golf
7 S. Dearborn St., Chicago, Ill.   Chrysler Bldg., New York

Fairyland Manufacturing Co. of California
1050 Cahuenga Street, Los Angeles, California

To Everybody: Watch for the Tom Thumb Course in your city. Play it just once and you'll want to play every day.

Above is a typical view showing part of the 18 hole Tom Thumb Golf Course.

To the left is a close-up of No. 1 hole of the Tom Thumb Golf Course.

The above pictures, including the one at the top of the page, indicate but several of the numerous ways in which Tom Thumb Golf can be laid out.

Diagram to the right shows a typical 18 hole layout which can go on a piece of property 120 feet by 120 feet, or any piece of somewhat similar dimensions.

The Saturday Evening Post, May 3, 1930, p.164

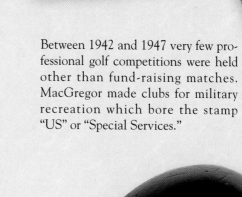

WWII wooden golf ball
used more so in Great Britain
The wooden golf ball took its
place in history as golfers placed
the dot on the ball correctly as to
orient the grain so not to break it.
c. 1943
approximate value $250.00

Between 1942 and 1947 very few professional golf competitions were held
other than fund-raising matches.
MacGregor made clubs for military
recreation which bore the stamp
"US" or "Special Services."

This Interview
was given to

Frazier Hunt

Associate Editor
of
Cosmopolitan
in
Europe
*whose ranch
adjoins that
of the Prince
in Canada*

The Prince of Wales

In the FIRST Interview

He ever Granted

Advocates Settling any

Disputes

between His Country *and*

Ours *on the* GOLF LINKS

IN August Cosmopolitan the Prince of Wales—who, since the illness of his father, has become the most significant figure in British affairs—discusses informally Anglo-American relations. You see a brand-new Prince, thinking deeply about great problems.

Be among those 1,600,000 intelligent families who keep well informed by reading Cosmopolitan. The August issue also contains a new installment of Calvin Coolidge's autobiography.

August *Hearst's International* Now on Sale

combined with

Cosmopolitan

A Class Magazine with more than 1,600,000 circulation

August 1929 Good Housekeeping

Good Housekeeping, August 1929
Would that it was so simple to come to such peaceful resolutions with all our international disputes. After WWII the new mechanized production techniques, new metals, and other inventive processes developed during the war were brought to play in the golf equipment industry. The time of the "classic" club era began.

Golf Collectors Society

The Golf Collectors Society is an international organization dedicated to preserving the treasures and traditions of the game of golf. Founded in 1970 by Robert Kuntz and Joseph S.F. Murdoch, the organization today has over 2,300 members from 18 different countries. The philosophy of the society was and has always remained "a not for profit fraternal organization that encourages members to visit, share information, and to establish friendships based on a common interest — the love of golf."

The GCS unites those who have a love for the game of golf and its artifacts. Members collect hickory shafted golf clubs, balls, books, tees, ceramics, silver, art, programs, postcards, early golf magazines, and autographs to name just a few. If it was used in the game of golf or portrays the game of golf, it's likely a GCS member collects it!

GCS members come from all walks of life. Tour and club pros, notable golf writers, the curators of the world's most prominent golf museums, the guy who lives down the block, all share in the same common interest — golf and all of the memorabilia associated with it.

Membership in the GCS brings many benefits. Each member receives our magazine, *The Bulletin*, published on a quarterly basis. It includes golf history, featured collections and collectors, book reviews, unusual clubs and artifacts, and general news on society doings. Each member also receives a membership directory, issued twice each year. Members are also welcome to attend the frequent regional meetings held in every part of the country, as well as the annual meeting, held yearly in the early fall.

For information about membership, contact

Golf Collectors Society
P.O. Box 241042
Cleveland, OH 44124
Phone: 440-460-3979
E-mail: www.golfcollectors.com

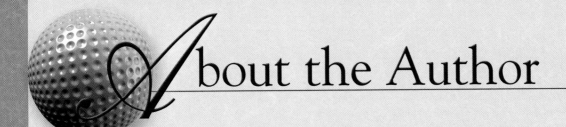

About the Author

Having worked all his life to be outstanding in whatever he does, author Ron John jokingly admits that his pursuit of excellence in sports has paid college tuition for several X-ray and CAT scan technicians. After serving six years in the United States Air Force from cadet to captain and earning doctorate and post doctorate degrees in special education and clinical psychology, Ron continued to challenge himself and contributed strongly as a builder and administrator of residential psychiatric centers in the western United States. His passion for sports has been rechanneled since 1996 because of back fusion surgery and firm doctor's orders into studying the history of golf and golfing equipment and collecting post WWI clubs. This book is another sound example of his desire to excel. His e-mail address is rorajohn@aol.com.

Index

Index

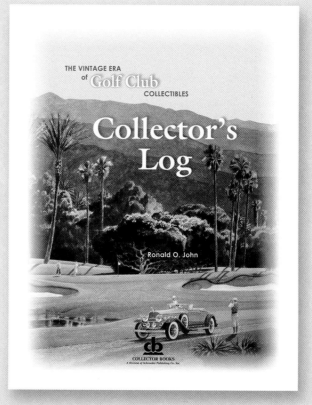

The Vintage Era of Golf Club Collectibles
Collector's Log

Ronald O. John

Author Ronald O. John has produced a companion collector's log to his *The Vintage Era of Golf Club Collectibles*. This log helps collectors do just that — log their finds. Arranged alphabetically by manufacturer, the book leaves space to list each set of clubs, then numbers for each wood and/or iron that can be circled as you acquire the various clubs. It can be used for both vintage and modern collectible clubs. The author prefaces the log with a grading scale as well as pricing information and basic guidelines for collectors.

#6010 • 8½ x 11 • 48 pgs. • PB • $9.95